OECD PROCEED

G000137916

Corporate Governance, State-Owned Enterprises and Privatisation

ORGANISATION FOR ECONOMIC CO-OPERATION AND DEVELOPMENT

ORGANISATION FOR ECONOMIC CO-OPERATION AND DEVELOPMENT

Pursuant to Article 1 of the Convention signed in Paris on 14th December 1960, and which came into force on 30th September 1961, the Organisation for Economic Co-operation and Development (OECD) shall promote policies designed:

– to achieve the highest sustainable economic growth and employment and a rising standard of living in Member countries, while maintaining financial stability, and thus to contribute to the development of the world economy;
– to contribute to sound economic expansion in Member as well as non-member countries in the process of economic development; and
– to contribute to the expansion of world trade on a multilateral, non-discriminatory basis in accordance with international obligations.

The original Member countries of the OECD are Austria, Belgium, Canada, Denmark, France, Germany, Greece, Iceland, Ireland, Italy, Luxembourg, the Netherlands, Norway, Portugal, Spain, Sweden, Switzerland, Turkey, the United Kingdom and the United States. The following countries became Members subsequently through accession at the dates indicated hereafter: Japan (28th April 1964), Finland (28th January 1969), Australia (7th June 1971), New Zealand (29th May 1973), Mexico (18th May 1994), the Czech Republic (21st December 1995), Hungary (7th May 1996), Poland (22nd November 1996) and Korea (12th December 1996). The Commission of the European Communities takes part in the work of the OECD (Article 13 of the OECD Convention).

FOREWORD

This publication contains the proceedings from a conference that was conducted on "State-Owned Enterprises, Privatisation and Corporate Governance" in Paris in March 1997. This meeting was one in a series of discussions conducted by the OECD Privatisation Network, a forum for the exchange of views on policy issues in privatisation.

Corporate governance is often defined as the interaction between owners and managers in controlling and directing a company. Different countries have different systems of governance which reflect their legal and institutional frameworks, historical practice and the structure and function of their financial markets. Apart from focusing on different models of corporate governance, the OECD has explored how private sector governance structures can improve the management and performance of state-owned enterprises and how different privatisation methods could impact post-privatisation governance structures and performance.

This publication examines these issues and provides some policy recommendations for the enhancement of corporate governance in public enterprises. It starts with a meeting summary, and an introductory paper that provides the overall context for the meeting. It proceeds to address corporate governance in state-owned enterprises in New Zealand, the use of public sector holding companies in Canada, and stable shareholders groups (noyaux dur) and cross-shareholdings in French privatisation. General governance issues in the context of public offerings and employee participation in privatisation are also analysed.

The opinions expressed in these papers are solely those of the individual authors and do not necessarily reflect the views of the OECD or the Governments of its Member countries. This volume is published on the responsibility of the Secretary-General of the OECD.

TABLE OF CONTENTS

OVERVIEW

In the context of its advisory work in corporate governance and privatisation, the OECD held a two day meeting entitled "State-Owned Enterprises, Privatisation and Corporate Governance" in Paris, on 3-4 March 1997. The purpose of this meeting was two-fold:

- to identify the main issues related to corporate governance structures and decision making mechanisms within state-owned enterprises (SOEs) and the main policy alternatives for addressing them;

- to analyse the effects of different privatisation policies and methods on corporate governance in privatised enterprises.

The meeting permitted senior officials and policy makers working in the areas of state-property management and enterprise reform with insight into different governance approaches for SOEs. A number of important conclusions were reached.

Main conclusions

- The weaknesses of governance in state-owned enterprises stem from insufficient market incentives and disciplines. There is no market for corporate control, *e.g.* no threat of take-over and replacement of incumbent management, shareholder exit is not possible and monitoring of performance by the state equity-holder is weak mainly due to the lack of economic motivation. Corporate governance is exercised by a chain of agents without identifiable principals.

- There is no credible threat of bankruptcy as SOEs are frequently bailed out. Accounting and disclosure generally do not meet private sector standards.

7

- Privatisation has obvious advantages when the firms in question serve primarily commercial functions. Nevertheless, SOEs are often used to serve non-commercial objectives, *e.g.* social cohesion, income redistribution, universal access to services. Serving conflicting objectives is a source of inefficiency. In many cases, public interest functions can be better accommodated by means other than public ownership, such as regulation in the case of natural monopolies, direct subsidies or long-term contracts.

- Despite their short-comings, SOEs are likely to continue to be an important part of the state's assets in many countries. It is therefore important to identify best practises for SOE corporate governance on the basis of comparative experience in OECD countries .

SOEs and governance techniques

- One approach to improving economic efficiency of SOEs is to **emulate private sector incentives**. This includes corporatisation of SOEs, *i.e.* their constitution as private law commercial entities, and creating transparency in the relationship between the State and the Board of Directors of the SOE, including a clear set of rules for the appointment of directors and a clear definition of the corporate goals. This also includes better monitoring and reporting for SOEs. Most importantly, SOEs should be subject to financial discipline. The State should not be seen as a guarantor of their liabilities; and its contribution to their capital should be transparent.

- **Performance contracts** between SOEs and the State are another way to exercise governance, especially in industries that are monopolistic. These contracts have evolved since the 1970s to include fewer production targets, clearer financial relationships -- especially with respect to future dividends -- and sufficient appreciation of management's need for flexibility in reacting to market changes.

- **Contracting out** the management of companies **to private sector** teams is another way to introduce private sector incentives. Such contracts require 1) explicit goals and objectives, 2) mutual

commitments from the state and the contractor and 3) m
with rewards and penalties.

- **Holding companies** were initially thought of as a way to
introduce private sector governance techniques in SOEs.
Experience however has shown that the costs associated with
them are usually greater than the benefits. The former may
include an additional layer of bureaucracy between owners and
management, loss of accountability and transparency, and the
danger of "regulatory capture" of holding company management.
Holding companies function well when their objectives are narrow
and limited in time, notably during periods of restructuring and
privatisation.

Privatisation and governance

- The need to provide for a stable corporate governance
environment for privatised firms should not result in the
preservation of insider privileges and the "status quo". The use of
cross-shareholdings and other devices to prevent control from
outside shareholders may considerably reduce the actual gains
from privatisation; they also risk reducing flexibility in the
corporate sector as a whole and may delay the structural
adjustment necessary in the context of globalisation.

- **Transparency** is at the heart of a successful privatisation process
and an effective post-privatisation governance environment. The
lack of it can result in increased political and social costs, by
making the selection of buyers less efficient and undermining
public confidence in the integrity of the process.

- Very often, governance structures are reshuffled in **preparation
for privatisation.** New boards, management and monitoring
mechanism are installed. However, when strategic majority
investors are anticipated to take over via trade sales, such
extensive managerial and governance restructuring might prove to
be redundant. It is usually more efficient to let new owners
perform these tasks.

- Sales to **majority strategic investors** might facilitate the
emergence of more effective governance arrangements but,

9

contrary to what is often thought, they do not automatically cure agency problems. In fact, monitoring and control procedures devised by strategic investors (usually large corporations) for internal purposes might be ill-adapted to address problems of strategy and management at the privatised company.

– **Initial public offerings** are the most transparent method of privatisation. They are also efficient from a governance perspective, provided that the equity markets are deep enough and the market for corporate control is functioning. Sometimes governments have created obstacles to take-overs, which might make policing by the market very difficult. Moreover, in many cases regulators might retain important governance functions in privatised companies by setting prices or targets for performance.

STATE OWNERSHIP, CORPORATE GOVERNANCE AND PRIVATISATION

by
Saul Estrin[*]

1.   Introduction

Privatisation has become a central plank in the global move towards more competitive market economies. During the 1970s, state owned firms accounted for more than 10 per cent of GDP in many of the leading OECD economies, including Britain, France, Italy and Austria. Today that figure has fallen sharply, and the concept of privatisation has spread to developing economies as well as the former communist regimes of Central and Eastern Europe [see Vickers and Yarrow (1988), Estrin (1994)].[1] These developments reflect a widespread dissatisfaction with the state as an owner of enterprises. It is argued that the state has been unable to motivate the firms in its portfolio to attain competitive standards in terms of efficiency, productivity, innovation, and orientation towards the consumer (see *e.g.* Peacock, 1984). There has also been considerable concern about the blurring of political and business objectives in state owned firms, especially in monopolies. In the first part of this paper, we explore the problems of corporate governance in state owned firms, and the main criteria determining good performance.

The lengthy experiments with alternative governance mechanisms for state owned firms led to a view that the persistent deficiencies of state ownership could best be addressed by privatisation. At this point, two further questions need to be addressed. The first are the prospects for improved enterprise performance, national economic competitiveness and other social objectives opened up by the privatisation policy. For example, the fact that the government has decided to privatise some significant companies allows the authorities also to pursue policies to induce foreign direct investment, *e.g.* for

*   London Business School, Sussex Place, Regents Park, London NW1 4SA, England. Not to be quoted without permission of the author.

access to advanced technologies, or to encourage worker share ownership, *e.g.* by providing discounts for employees or for small shareholders. The second concerns the methods of privatisation, focusing on three broad categories - public offerings, sales to strategic investors and employee buyouts. Each has different implications for the corporate governance problem, and these differences themselves depend on other factors such as technology, sector and scale. We approach these issues in the latter part of the paper.

In the subsequent section, we outline the corporate governance problem in general, and the way it is addressed in public and private sector firm. We use this to derive the key criteria to evaluate corporate governance mechanisms in state owned firms. Implications for privatisation are drawn in the third section, which also considers the role of market structure, and competition policy in assessing privatisation policies. A brief comparison of the strengths and weaknesses of alternative governance mechanisms is drawn in the fourth section, which looks in particular at the strengths and weaknesses of employee ownership. Conclusions are drawn in the fifth section.

2.   **A comparison of corporate governance in state owned and private firms**

Firms owned and run by their founding entrepreneur (or his or her successors), are thought by economists to have relatively few problems of enterprise objectives and managerial incentives. The objective of the firm in this case can be thought of as profit maximisation, to be attained either in the short or longer run, while incentive problems do not arise because ownership and control are concentrated in the same individual. The problem of corporate governance arises when ownership and control are separated, for example between shareholders and managers. The owners bear the residual risk and receive the residual reward, but it is the managers who control the decision-making process and therefore make all the decisions which influence those risks and rewards. The two parties may have different objectives or react differently the different circumstances. Even with private ownership, it is not hard to imagine circumstances in which managers divert the resources of the firm from the task of rewarding shareholders to the gratification of their own interests, for example through managerial perks, salaries, offices, executive jets and so forth.

It is important to stress that this problem arises from two factors: - because of the fact that managers and owners have different objectives and because the owner does not have complete information about the behaviour and decisions of the manager. The issue is an example of the "agency" problem [see *e.g.* Alchian and Demsetz (1972), Jensen and Meckling (1976), Hart (1995)], in which the "principal" - the owner - seeks an efficient way to ensure that the "agent" - management - acts in the principal's rather than the agent's best interest. When the principal does not have full information about the circumstances and decision-making of the agent, they must design a contract between them which provides the agent with appropriate incentives, punishes its unsatisfactory behaviour and which can be successfully monitored. This paper is concerned with the different factors conducive to successful monitoring in state owned and private enterprises, as well as between different forms of private enterprises.

The "principal-agent" problem described above is a completely general one, but in this paper we focus on its application in state owned versus private firms. The differences therefore apply to the objectives of the principal (private owner or state) and the agent (managers in private and public firms). Moreover it must be stressed that if information were perfect and complete contracts could be written, it would make no difference whether firms were in private or state hands, because either type of owner could enforce their objectives upon the management. Differences of behaviour derive from the different governance structures and monitoring systems under the two forms of ownership and these differences may be complex and depend upon institutional structures and administrative traditions as well as the nature of specific owner-management contracts.

In the remainder of this section, we outline an idealised view of how corporate governance works in the private sector, to contrast it with the parallel mechanisms of state owned firms. The additional complexity of the governance relationship under public ownership is highlighted. In subsequent sections, we add some important provisos to our picture of private ownership, which inform our later analysis of privatisation.

2.1. Governance in the private sector

In the privately owned corporation, the informational and incentives structures are usually described as follows. Managers are paid to maximise profit for owners, but are assumed also to pursue prestige and power; for example to try to increase their benefits and to promote company growth at the expense of profit [Williamson (1963, 1980)]. Stockholders bear most of the risk, but cannot observe managers' actions directly. They are kept informed of the company's performance by regularly published accounts and through the share price [Millward and Parker (1983)]. The company can also be compared with others in the same sector to "benchmark" the impact of external events on its performance.

Four types of sanctions and incentives are used to induce managers to maximise profit. First, the market for shares gives owners a means of pressure, since they can withdraw their assets by selling stock. Shareholders have incentives to monitor managers, and the trading associated with the stock market and reflected in the share price, allows the emergence of a "common expectation" about the future yields of the firm relative to the industry. Moreover, the existence of outside shareholders also provides a mechanism of sanction against poorly performing managers. Managers may be dismissed if a lower share price leads to takeovers by outsiders attracted to make profits by replacing the management team [Manne (1965)]. The threat of bankruptcy with its consequent damage to their reputation may also discipline managers. Finally, even when their remuneration takes the form of a salary, the managerial market makes present and future emoluments depend on performance [Fama (1980)]. Recently, managerial salaries have come increasingly to include significant performance bonuses and stock options.

These monitoring arrangements are only effective under certain conditions. Two cases of limitation on the owner's ability to obtain and use information are particularly relevant for a comparison with the public sector. The first is when share ownership is diffuse, with a large number of small stockholders. The problems of decision-making among numerous small shareholders are often seen as a problem of constructing a group utility function but this ignores the economies of scale present in matters of information and decision-making when information is costly. It may be too costly for a small shareholder to collect enough information to convince others of dismissing managers perceived to have unsatisfactory performance. Even though one shareholder's assets may be shifted to a different venture, this is unlikely to have a significant influence on the operation of the company. This is clearly relevant in considering the appropriate form of ownership, post-privatisation.

The second restriction factor has to do with market structure. With a small number of large firms, comparison with other companies in the same sector becomes more uncertain and the informational advantage to management greater. A monopolistic structure therefore reinforces informational asymmetry and managers' opportunities to pursue their own objectives, while competition reduces it, whether ownership is public or private.

2.2.   Governance in the public sector

In many countries, it has been recognised that business operations, even if publicly owned, have to be run according to a commercial rather than an administrative cycle.   This implies that day-to-day management of public corporations is typically independent. Thus, the state is the main (and often the only) shareholder, and makes a contract with management to ensure public sector objectives are pursued. However, as Alchain and Demsetz (1972) stress, there are no tradeable claims to the state's ownership right, which causes problems for monitoring and underlies the perception of public sector inefficiency. The argument goes as follows. The state owns public sector firms but, in the absence of a market for public corporation stock, does not have the possibility to evaluate performance by following share price fluctuations.

The share price represents a conflagration of different expectations. Different agents with diverse attitudes towards current performance and future prospects buy and sell shares according to the divergence between their expectations and the current market price. As long as these expectations are formed independently the ruling share price emerges via a pooling of information, and represents a more thorough and diffuse monitoring than could be undertaken by a single agency. However efficient the state's monitoring activities, they will be inferior to the private market.

The absence of a market for shares similarly removes sanctions for bad performance and incentives to managers in the public sector. Civil servants, who are not entitled to the gains due to improved efficiency, have no financial incentive to monitor public firms. Members of the public do not have the possibility of shifting their assets away from unprofitable ventures, lowering share prices and informing potential bidders that the companies' assets are not earning the maximum possible return. The absence of shareholders' rebellions or takeovers removes a crucial check on public sector performance, leaving management far more discretion than in the case of private ownership [see Lindsay (1980), Kay and Silberston (1984), Millward and Parker (1983)]). Public corporations are sometimes even thought to have a `soft budget constraint' [Kornai (1980)] with virtually unlimited access to government funds, so the company runs no risk of bankruptcy, no matter how inefficient its management. The absence of tradeable shares also rules out incentive schemes tying management remuneration in part to the performance of the firm via the share price, for example through share option plans. One must presume that all this can lead to excessive slack in nationalised corporations (de Alessi, 1980). Management may also take advantage of deficient monitoring to shirk their

15

duties and let trade unions appropriate a larger share of company rents in the form of high wages and overemployment (see, *e.g.*, Pryke, 1981).

This "property rights" approach puts great stress on ownership rights and monitoring arrangements, but places little emphasis on the possibility that public sector owners may have objectives other than profit maximisation. Nationalisations, the bulk of which took place after the Second World War in Western Europe, were originally approved by voters as `being in the national interest', even if that involved some relaxation of market pressures. Other goals were also stressed at the time, including universality of service, income redistribution, consumer representation and more `social' employment policies. The correction of market failures by controlling natural monopolies and assisting in financing lumpy investments was also raised in the debate.

The potential multiplicity of goals emerging from the political process introduces difficulties in measuring the degree of target fulfilment, especially when objectives are defined as loose long-term goals. In the absence of agreement on the operational implications of general policy, the degree to which the public interest is met is not easily defined. One potential difficulty is that some of the objectives may actually conflict with each other. For example, breaking even may be impossible with price restrictions, or long-term competitiveness may require heavy borrowing for low return investments.

Furthermore, the way that public sector objectives are formulated leads one to expect that they may be frequently changed. The standard framework suggests that the public sector will receive targets consistent with those of the `median voter; as perceived by politicians (Millward and Parker, 1983). These will accommodate specific interest groups if these have a key role in the outcome of the elections and therefore be frequently changed in line with opinion poll evaluations of the median voter's preferences. Public sector resources may also be used by the incumbent government to their short-term political advantage, as a source of patronage and to settle political scores. All this will generate a tendency for the government to intervene constantly and unsystematically in the management of nationalised corporations, (see Littlechild, 1981).

Frequent changes in managerial objectives create confusion. The changes may be faster than is required for the results of the corresponding policies to become apparent - at least, managers will be able to claim so. As in the case of vague or contradictory goals, the outcome of managers' decisions ends up unobservable. The ability of the principal to draw a contract with an agent whose actions cannot be constantly monitored crucially depends on the visibility of the resulting performance. The more complex or variable the objectives, the higher the information and monitoring costs to the principle. Unobservable results greatly increase management's informational advantage, opening opportunities for 'hidden action'.

Estrin and Perotin (1987) sought to bring these points together in a unified framework which stressed the differences in both objectives and contractual arrangements between the public and private sectors. As we have seen, in private firms, shareholders commission management to maximise profit, and draw on the devices of the capital market, as well as bankruptcy and takeover legislation, to provide appropriate incentives. In contrast, the objectives of public corporations are defined via the political process, and transmitted through the state's own administrative structure to managers. Thus there is a chain of principals and agents from the voters to the managers of public sector firms, and these additional contractual tiers make the control of public sector managers more complex than in the private sector. The chains of principal and agent are contrasted in Table 1.

Table 1

Private Sector	Shareholders		Managers
Public Sector	Voters	→	State Apparatus → Public Sector Managers
			Governments → Civil Service

We noted above the complexity in monitoring that may arise because public sector objectives in firms were non-economic, inconsistent and frequently changing. This arises from the way these objectives were formed by the voting process. Table 1 also covers the possibility that the firm may not take account of all politically-defined goals which it has been instructed to pursue. Different constitutional systems allow them different degrees of direct influence on actual policy implementation. Moreover the implementation of policies chosen by the governing party or coalition can be modified in any country by inertia or tradition. However, there are institutional and constitutional characteristics which make a system more or less responsive to political interventions, and thus affect the implementation of policies. Consider the case of an administrative structure which is, *de facto*, autonomous, making decisions on the public sector without reference to the political process. Problems associated with inconsistent or constantly changing objectives would never arise and public sector behaviour would be determined by the interaction between the goals of civil servants and public managers.

2.3. *Implications for corporate governance structures in the public sector*

The approach summarised in Table 1 suggests that the appropriateness of alternative monitoring structures will depend on:

i) the nature and consistency of objectives of the State as owner of business enterprises, which will in part relate to the political process;

ii) the internal structures of the government apparatus;

iii) the relationship between the civil service and managers as specified by the particular governance structure;

iv) the other market factors, notably the competitiveness of the product market and the public sector managerial market.

In this section, we consider two alternative public sector organisations and governance structures, ranging in level of autonomy from government departments through series of autonomous public corporations. (See Parris, Pestieau and Saynar, 1987).

a) *Direct state management*

This usually takes the form of departments or agencies under direct budgetary control. When the state manages directly, the agency problem is transferred to the relationship between elected and administrative branches at government. Direct management is a way for the state to circumvent the risk of hidden action. As such, it is particularly appropriate in cases where the objective of public ownership is vague and open to interpretation. This is often associated with the characteristics of the product, for example when output is difficult to measure, or consumers have little way of determining the adequacy of the supplied actions, like in health or education.

b) Public corporations

Activities that require medium-term investment and flexibility of response to market signals may not be good cases for civil servant management. More or less autonomous corporations have been set up to ensure that operations that had to be run according to a productive and commercial rather than administrative cycle would enjoy sufficient independence in day-to-day management.

Public corporations are typically found in industrial or extractive activities. The corporation is 100 per cent state-owned, and the majority of the board members are appointed by the government. Corporate finances are separate from the government budget, although the company may be allowed to borrow or invest on the private market. While statutory obligations restrict the options available to management, varying degrees of autonomy are granted in matters like employment and wages. Otherwise, corporate strategy is in principle autonomous. Corporate accounts are subject to normal administrative control and to Parliamentary scrutiny.

In the public corporation, the state therefore has all the powers associated with ownership of capital. It is in the position of a single shareholder, and does not need to form coalitions to impose sanctions. However, there are problems in monitoring management's performance. If the corporation operates in a competitive environment, comparison with other firms in the same industry provides a reference for evaluating technical efficiency and devising selective compensation schemes. Furthermore, institutional networks of competence, such as the French grand *corps* (see Suleiman, 1978) may provide the relevant ministry with inside information as well as expert 'second opinions' on public sector performance. Such networks can be seen as non-market alternatives to internalising agency relations by means of mergers and vertical integration. This could be particularly useful if the corporation has monopoly power. Like private shareholders, the state can also learn from its long association with industrial operations [Radner (1986)].

In certain cases, one could imagine state monitoring could be as effective as capital market monitoring. Provided the state can substitute for stock market information by mechanisms of benchmarking, the remaining requirement is that corporate objectives transmitted to the firm are clear and stable. However, if the objectives remain 'fuzzy', a high degree of monitoring may be required, with increased detailed instructions and close *ex-ante* control of activities. The less well defined the objective, the more necessary and the more attractive to the government it becomes to specify and monitor management's actions rather than outcomes. Public corporations subject to this type of control have a much reduced autonomy. But evaluating performance is impossible in situations where *a priori* options are unknown to the monitor, and the costs of even imperfect monitoring are likely to be prohibitive. Full monitoring amounts to transferring responsibility onto the monitoring body, leaving in effect a large degree of discretion to the agent by not defining, and hence not limiting the agent's areas of discretion. Similarly, frequent redefinitions of objectives require more intervention into the day-today running of the public sector. This in turn makes management more likely to deny any responsibility for the results, while their actual behaviour further escapes observation.

A possible solution to these problems is the widespread use of planning agreements or planning contracts. These are signed after negotiations between public sector managers and administrators, and link corporate finance, grants and managerial incentives to the achievement of agreed *targets* over the medium term. Planning contracts allow both parties to exchange information and harmonise expectations. An agency contract may be drawn, in sources to assess public sector managers' performance. However, planning contracts carry the risk of adverse selection, when managers use hidden (or inside) information to set targets that are more consistent with their own goals than with the efficient pursuit of government objectives. Contracts are necessarily incomplete, and the existence of the contract then restricts later corrective intervention (Bazex, 1984). The better the sources of information available to the state, the less the risk.

In summary, when well-defined and stable objectives are given to public corporations, government monitoring of their performance could, in principle, be as effective as capital market monitoring. Indeed, there are a few situations (*e.g.*, diffuse private share ownership, undeveloped stock market monopolies, long-term public ownership) in which the government may have access to more information and stronger powers to sanction bad performance than private shareholders. However in practice government objectives are unlikely to be purely financial and the sources of information available to civil servants about managerial performance is likely to be inferior to that obtained via a stock market. Moreover, managers will have even more discretion if unclear or changing goals are transmitted to the firm because of the political process, or if the firm 'captures' the relevant agency.

3.   Corporate governance and privatisation

Vickers and Yarrow (1988) argue that, while the record of public sector ownership in the UK from the Second World War to 1979 was poor for reasons of inherent deficiencies in the ownership structures and monitoring arrangements, there remained the possibility of substantial improvements in performance by altering the control system.   They recommended in particular mechanisms to distance ministers from managers and improved incentives for internal efficiency, including the development of an agency devoted to monitoring performance and performance-related pay schemes for public sector management.   In practice however, the Thatcher government chose instead to privatise the bulk of nationalised firms rather than to improve public sector governance.   Privatisation brought some new issues to the fore, notably the sharp distinction in monitoring arrangements between competitive and monopolistic industries under private ownership.   While highly relevant for decades in the US and elsewhere (see *e.g.* Kahn, 1970), this important distinction was blurred for state owned enterprises because the government rarely explicitly regulated natural monopolies in a manner differently than other enterprises.

3.1.   A residual role for the State?

Consider the case of a firm operating in a competitive industry in an economy with a large efficient stock exchange. In this situation, there is little to be said about corporate governance post-privatisation -the authorities will seek to turn the former state owned enterprise into a private firm, monitored by its shareholders according to the mechanisms outlined in section 2.1.   This assumes that the authorities do not have additional objectives sought through the privatisation, such as wider employee ownership.   Examples of such privatisations in the UK include Amersham International, Jaguar and Rolls Royce.

The most significant exception to this analysis arises when the public firm in question is a natural monopoly, operating in a market not capable of offering adequate competitive pressure. Privatisation can be an effective way of increasing company orientation to profits, with potentially powerful consequences for cost cutting, efficiency enhancement and increases in consumer satisfaction (see *e.g.* Bos, 1986). However, these improvements in the internal efficiency of firms may be more than offset by a deterioration in allocative efficiency if the newly privatised firm operates in non-competitive markets. This is because the unfettered monopoly power of privately owned profit-maximising firms is well understood to lead to losses in consumer welfare and dead-weight losses, as well as sluggish performance with respect to consumers and to innovation.

The nature of the solution to this problem depends on the reason why monopoly power was conferred on the state owned firm originally. If the monopoly was granted and protected by statute as is generally true, for example, in Post Offices around the world, then competition could perhaps be ensured by combining privatisation with lowering barriers to entry. Similarly, firms created or merged into a monopoly for strategic reasons, as might be the case for railway systems, could be broken up into competing units. Firms which were originally granted a monopoly, but which now, because of technical change, could support the entry of new competitors, could be brought face to face with entrants by liberalisation, and perhaps even some degree of support for new entrants. In general, in situations where competition is feasible, it should be encouraged and supported, both to provide pressure on monopoly profits and to provide benchmarking information about relative performance.

However, there is one situation in which opening the market up to entry and competition will not be enough to ensure that privatisation yields allocative efficiency. This is when the public sector firm in question is a natural monopoly. In this case, the authorities will need to supplement privatisation with a contractual system and monitoring arrangement to ensure that the newly privatised enterprise does not abuse its monopoly power. This is probably best achieved through a formal system of regulation which would substitute for the absence of competitive pressures from other firms.

The agency problems faced by regulatory authorities are similar to the more general issues of corporate governance by the state owned enterprises. There are informational asymmetries between regulators and firms, and of course the two parties have different objectives. In devising regulatory structures, American and British experience highlights the role of independent regulatory authorities formed to monitor the attainment of publicly determined targets for the private sector monopolies.

In summary, there is little need for any residual role for state in corporate governance post-privatisation, provided capital markets are well developed and product markets are competitive. However, the authorities will need to maintain a governance role over natural monopolies. The principal-agent literature suggests that this will be most effectively achieved through an independent regulatory authority, empowered to intervene in a non-discretionary manner to prevent monopolistic abuses.

3.2.   Objectives of privatisation and corporate governance

From Britain to Russia, the fundamental aim of privatisation has been to improve corporate performance. However, privatisation is a policy with multiple objectives, the satisfaction of which has implications for the resulting system of corporate governance. The simplest example concerns the financial motive for privatisation, and how that conflicts with policies for liberalisation and regulatory control. From the very first privatisations in the UK in 1981, an important objective was to raise revenues in order to reduce public sector deficit or to repay the National Debt. This means that Ministry of Finance officials sought the highest possible price for their asset, which in turn depended on their future profitability. However, the more competitive the environment into which the newly privatised company was placed, and the more rigorous the regulatory regime to which it was subjected, the lower the asking prices would have to be.

There are two further examples of policy objectives of privatisation with particular relevance to the subsequent system of corporate governance. The first concerns access to new technology or to more sophisticated managerial know-how. For example in many countries in Central and Eastern Europe, foreign ownership is seen as virtually the only way to upgrade the technological capacity and international competitiveness of domestic industry. Hungary has been particularly successful in this respect, with some 20 per cent of investment since 1990 having been funded by foreign investors. Foreign direct investment has also been closely associated with privatisation in developing economies. According to Cook and Kirkpatrick (1995), foreign exchange represented about 30 per cent of total privatisation revenues in developing countries between 1988 and 1992; interestingly it is privatisation in Africa and to a lower extent Latin America which has relied most intensively on foreign investors. It is domestic investors who have provided the vast bulk of funds in East Asia however. In situations where domestic capital is scarce and capital markets are thin and underdeveloped, governments may be wise to abandon hierarchial control by local politicians in favour of hierarchial control within Western multinational corporations.

Privatisation policy in many countries has also been associated with the government's desire to promote wider share ownership. In the British case, the motives were largely political - to create a wider class of property owners - and such ambitions were echoed from 1990 in the transitional economies of Central and Eastern Europe (see Estrin,1994). There are two distinct forms of this policy. The first is to encourage shareholding among the population as a whole, for example by offering significant discounts in the sale price to individuals purchasing relatively modest blocks of shares. The concept was taken to an extreme in the (former) Czechoslovakia, where vouchers were distributed at very low cost to the entire adult population, enabling them to participate in world's first "mass privatisation" of more than 1 400 companies. The second is to sell (or give) the public firm to the labour force, either on their own (an employee buyout - EBO) or jointly with management (a manager-employee buyout - MEBO). This was undertaken in the UK with the privatisation by MEBO of National Freight Corporation in 1982. More recently, the Russian mass privatisation of 1993, though notionally based on vouchers on Czechoslovak lines, in fact offered such financial advantages to insiders that MEBO - type privatisation predominated (see World Bank, *Development Report,* 1996). According to Earle and Estrin (1996), employees obtained control in some 85 per cent of Russian privatisations; the average holding of insiders exceeded 65 per cent in privatised firms.

Clearly, policies of this sort lead governments to consider a variety of privatisation forms, and therefore of corporate governance systems post-privatisation. In particular, we have noted that there will be tensions between the desire to draw on domestic capital market information and benchmarks as against the need to attract foreign capital, technology and knowhow. Similarly, pressure for worker share ownership or employee control detract from the need, stressed in Section 2 above, to ensure that ownership on domestic capital markets is not too diffuse to prevent effective corporate governance. We return to these issues in the following section.

4.   Corporate governance in privatised firms

We argued above that if capital markets are well developed and efficient; product (and perhaps managerial) markets are competitive; and the government's objective in privatisation is to raise corporate efficiency, then the appropriate way to privatise is by public offerings. The resulting corporate governance mechanism should have the properties discussed in Section 2.1 above. However, these conditions are not always fulfilled, especially in less developed or transitional economies. In that case, if the expected benefits of privatisation still outweigh the option value of continued state ownership[2], the government will need to consider other modes of privatisation. We here consider trade sales to strategic investors and sales to employees.

Sales to strategic investors will be of particular relevance when capital markets are underdeveloped, so that the government would not be able to rely on the stock market fulfilling its key role in corporate governance. It may also be useful in situations where corporate governance has been particularly weak, because it ensures sufficient concentration of ownership for the prospect of effective governance in the future. This argument is strengthened when the buyers bring complementary skills and experience in the relevant markets - for example the sale of the Royal Ordnance factories to British Aerospace in 1987. A specific example of this form of privatisation is sale to foreign direct investors, as discussed above.

The big danger with sales to strategic investors arise from the potential for monopolistic abuse. Interested domestic investors are likely to be competitors or private companies placed strategically up or downstream from the privatising company. They may be willing to offer the highest price, and to offer the capacity to restructure effectively, but the cost in terms of allocative efficiency may also be high. Even when the strategic investor is a foreign firm, governments should be wary of deals in which technological advantages are likely to confer a monopolitistic position on the restructrured privatised firm, or in which the foreign investor seeks to restrict trade in that product.

An alternative method of privatisation is by sale to the employees. There are many possible advantages to such a policy. It is widely argued that employee ownership is a unique form of corporate governance which can act to enhance productivity, by encouraging peer group monitoring, by improving employee motivation and by avoiding needless conflict (see Bonin, Putterman and Jones, 1993). Employee ownership may also assist in the turnaround of bankrupt firms, by increasing the scope for management-employee cooperation and by opening the possibility for wage concessions (see Bradley and Gelb, 1983).

However, there are also strong criticisms of employee ownership. According to Hansmann (1990), these arise because employees are heterogeneous in skills, interests and abilities, and employee owned firms must put in place mechanisms to resolve these conflicts. The potential productivity gains noted above are bought at a price; the time foregone in meetings that would not be necessary in an outsider-owned firm, or the consequence of poor or slow decision-making. For example, there may be different attitudes towards technical change between unskilled, skilled and white collar workers, or toward the benefits of internally financed investment between younger and older workers. The greater the heterogeneity, the greater the costs of reaching agreement, or of taking decisions which represent inefficient compromises. Hansmann concludes that employee ownership would operate best when employees are relatively less heterogeneous with respect to skills and jobs, and where firms are relatively small.

The second agency problem for employee owned firms arises when they need to finance investment externally either through debt or equity. Employee ownership opens up a fundamental problem for potential funders, namely that they are open to opportunistic behaviour. Minority equity holders cannot easily prevent worker owners from profits to themselves in higher wages. Lenders cannot prevent workers from decumulating assets to increase their consumption. This also probably explains the problems that employee owned firms have traditionally had in financing their investment externally, and the chronic under investment which has often resulted (see Bonin, Jones and Patterman, 1993).

This suggests that, despite the potential benefits on the productivity side, privatisation by sale to employees might sensibly be restricted to relatively small, labour-intensive firms, and perhaps to firms in declining sectors and regions (see Earle and Estrin, 1996).

5. Conclusion

This paper has sought briefly to review the issues in corporate governance comparing public sector and private firms. The argument is complex because, since the principal-agent structures are layered and hierarchical under state ownership, a number of factors, including political objectives and structures, organisational arrangements within the civil service and the monitoring arrangements for public corporations influence its effectiveness. However a number of key results stand out.

First, it is possible to run public sector firms more efficiently, perhaps even approaching the performance which could be attained under private ownership. For example, clarity of corporate objectives, clear lines of responsibility, independent agencies for monitoring and the greater use of competitive pressures and financial incentives can all play an important role in improving public sector performance, even in the absence of privatisation.

26

Secondly, privatisation needs to go hand in hand with liberalisation or, in the case of natural monopolies, with an effective regulatory system. This latter must clearly be independent of both the government and the firms, and must provide surrogate competition when successful entry by new private firms is not feasible.

Finally, the advantages of private ownership are traditionally deduced in circumstances when capital markets are sophisticated and can use the information contained in the share price to motivate managers and to trigger the threat of takeover. This would suggest that privatisation should take the form of public offering. However, there are circumstances, such as when capital markets are poorly developed, in which alternative forms of privatisation may be preferable. An obvious example is sale to a strategic partner, whether domestic or foreign, though it is important to guard against monopolistic abuse. An alternative is employee ownership which, though attractive in certain circumstances, should probably be limited to smaller-sized firms that are capable of internal financing.

NOTES

1.   According to the *Privatisation Yearbook*, the proceeds from privatisation sales amounted to a remarkable $135bn between 1988 and 1992. The bulk of the sales by value, unsurprisingly, were in industrialised countries, with Europe alone accounting for 56 per cent of the total, and up to 80 per cent in particular years. However the share of developing countries has been growing rapidly, from 6 per cent in 1988 to 42 per cent in 1992, with most privatisations occurring in South America (see Cook and Kirkpatrick, 1995). More recently the Czech, Slovaks and Russians have led the way in Central and Eastern Europe with so called "mass privatisation" schemes which have transferred ownership of firms supplying up to 60 per cent GDP from state to private hands [see Estrin (1994), World Bank *Development Report* (1996), EBRD *Transition Report*, 1996].

2.   For example the possibility of restructuring under state ownership prior to privatisation, permitting the state to reap the capital gains. This occured in the UK with British Steel.

REFERENCES

ALCHIAN, A.A. and H. DEMSETZ, Production, Information Costs and Economic Organization, *American Economic Review* 62, no. 5, 777-795, 1972.

BONIN, J., JONES, D.C. and PUTTERMAN, L., "Theoretical and Empirical Studies of Producer Cooperation": *Journal of Economic Literature*, Vol. 31, pp. 1290-1390, 1993.

BOS, D., *Public Enterprise Economics*, North-Holland, Amsterdam, 1986.

BRADLEY, K and GELB, A., *Cooperation at Work*, London: Heinemann 1983.

COOK, P. and KIRKPARTRICK, C., *Privatisation Policy and Performance: International Perspectives*, London, Prentice Hall, 1995.

EARLE, J.S., and ESTRIN, S., "Employee Ownership in Transition", LBS, CIS-ME Discussion paper 17, 1996.

EBRD, *Transition Report*, 1996.

ESTRIN , S., *Privatisation in Central and Eastern Europe*, London, Longmans, 1994.

ESTRIN, S. and PEROTIN V. "The Regulation of British and French Nationalised Industries", *European Economic Review*, Vol. 31 pp. 361-7, 1987.

FAMA, E., Agency Problems and the Theory of the Firm, *Journal of Political Economy* 88. 288-307, 1980.

HANSMANN, H. "When Does Worker Ownership Work?" *Yale Law Review*, Vol. 98, pp. 1751-816, 1990.

HART, O., *Firms, Contracts and Financial Structure*, Oxford: Oxford University Press, 1995.

JENSEN, M. and MECKLING, W., "Theory of the Firm: Managerial Behaviour, Agency Costs and Ownership Structure", *Journal of Financial Economics*, Vol. 3 pp. 305-60, 1976.

KAY, J.A. and Z.A. SILBERSTON, 1984, The New Industrial Policy - Privatisation and Competition, *Midland Bank Review*, Spring, 8-I6.

KAHN, A.E., *Economics of Regulation*, New York, Riley, 1970.

KORNAI, J., *The Economics of Shortage*, Amsterdam, North Holland, 1980.

LINDSAY, C., Is There a Theory of Public Organizations? in: Clarkson and Martin, ads., *The Economics of Nonproprietary Organizations*, New York, JAI Press, 1980.

MANNE, H.G., Mergers and the Market for Corporate Control, *Journal of Political Economy* 73, 110-120, 1965.

MILLWARD, R. and D.M. PARKER, Public and Private Enterprise: Comparative Behaviour an Relative Efficiency in: Millward *et al.*, *Public Sector Economics* (Macmillan, London), 1981.

PARRIS, H., P. PESTIEAU and P. SAYNOR, *Public Enterprise in Western Europe*, London, Croom Helm, 1987.

PEACOCK, H., 1984, Privatisation in perspective, *Three Banks Review* 144, Dec., 3-25.

PRYKE, R., *The Nationalised Industries. Policies and Performance since 1968*, Oxford, Martin Robertson.

RADNER, R., The Internal Economy of Large Firms, *Economic Journal* 96, Suppl., March, I-23, 1986.

SULEIMAN, E., *Elites in French Society*, Princeton, Princeton University Press, 1978.

VICKERS, J. and G. Yarrow, *Privatization*, London, MIT Press, 1988.

WILLIAMSON. O., Managerial discretion and business behavior. *American Economic Review,* 1963.

WILLIAMSON, O., The Organization of Work: A Comparative Institutional Assessment, *Journal of Economic and Business Organization*, 1980.

World Bank Development Report: *From Plan to Market*, Washington DC, 1996.

STATE OWNED ENTERPRISE GOVERNANCE:
FOCUS ON ECONOMIC EFFICIENCY

by
Jim Brumby and Michael Hyndman[*]

1.   Introduction

In New Zealand the central government continues to own a significant number of commercial businesses, despite substantial divestments in recent years. Most are structured as companies. These companies include 15 State Owned Enterprises (SOEs). A case may be made for privatising more SOEs. The basic argument is that governments are relatively poorly placed to manage commercial activities effectively. The nub of this argument is that government-owned companies such as SOEs typically have more serious agency problems than privately-owned companies. These problems include:

- weak external pressures from capital markets (for example, no threat of takeover), and often from product markets; and

- the political reasoning that produced public ownership often conflicts with economic efficiency.

Our concern is with the impact these problems have on economic efficiency in New Zealand, and thereby the welfare of New Zealanders. We do not consider distributional issues. Instead we adopt the premise that - once distributional policy decisions have been made - to achieve welfare goals will require the government's balance sheet (including SOEs) to be managed in the

*   Commercial and Financial Branch, New Zealand Treasury. The views in this paper represent the views of the authors, and should not be construed as being the views of the New Zealand Treasury.

The authors are grateful to Stuart Shepherd, a former Treasury colleague, who co-authored an earlier version of this paper, and to David Greig (another former Treasury colleague) and David Skilling for their comments on the paper.

most efficient way (in terms of provision, management and financing decisions).

For a variety of reasons, a sizeable number of commercial businesses may remain government owned. The focus of this paper, therefore, is on how to ensure that such companies - while remaining government-owned - make the best feasible contribution to economic efficiency in New Zealand. It examines policy measures for achieving this goal.

Section 2 of the paper provides contextual information to assist the reader in understanding the main SOE issues in New Zealand today. *Section 3* defines the basic problem which has prompted the focus of this paper. It includes a discussion of the characteristics of government ownership that are likely to reduce the economic efficiency of SOEs. *Section 4* proposes a set of measures for counteracting the weaknesses of government ownership of such businesses. It focuses on enhancing their contribution to economic efficiency. Finally, *Section 5* draws together the main conclusions about the policy proposed measures.

2.   Context of issues

2.1   *Economic efficiency and its importance*

In analysing the management of government-owned businesses (including their governance arrangements) we are interested in the extent to which their production, investment, financing and pricing decisions are economically efficient. We have in mind all three widely-used dimensions of economic efficiency: allocative, productive and dynamic. Allocative efficiency occurs when resources are attracted to the uses in which they are valued most. Productive efficiency occurs when goods or services are produced by the least cost method. Dynamic efficiency occurs when people (*e.g.* New Zealand citizens) have incentives to save, invest and consume in ways that, over a relevant time horizon, result in the maximum welfare for them in aggregate.

Our analysis starts from the premise that once the government has determined its distributional policy goals (*e.g.* as regards income, wealth and taxes), the extent to which the implementation of these policies is economically efficient can significantly affect New Zealander's aggregate welfare[1].

In the case of commercially oriented SOEs, maximising their value through time is taken as a proxy test for achieving their highest level of productive efficiency. It is also consistent with allocative efficiency where an SOE's product market is subject either to significant competition or a regulatory regime that effectively moderates any market dominance. In other words, where either of these conditions apply, aiming to maximise an SOE's value is likely to result in the SOE making the maximum contribution to economic efficiency possible under the constraints of government ownership. In view of the relatively greater agency problems associated with government ownership, however, the SOE is unlikely to be able to achieve the maximum possible level of economic efficiency.

In the interests of enhancing New Zealand's welfare, government needs to give priority to economic efficiency goals. This may lead to a decision to constrain the scope and scale of an SOE's business activities, or take action to increase the contestability of those activities.

2.2   Size and composition of SOEs

SOEs are a major component of both the central government's balance sheet and the wider economy. As at 30 June 1996 their assets of NZ$ 12.5 billion comprised 21% of the book value of total assets controlled by the government, SOEs and other government entities. They were equivalent to 28% of the asset book value of the New Zealand Stock Exchange top 40 group of companies. Their total revenue equated to 5.2% of GDP. SOEs control a diverse range of business activities. These include electricity generation and transmission, provision of postal and meteorological services, coal and forestry production, farm and office-building management, and control of domestic air traffic. How SOEs use the resources under their control, therefore, has a major impact on New Zealand's economic performance.[2]

2.3   Key players in the SOE sector

The equity shares in each SOE company are held jointly by the Minister of Finance and the Minister for State Owned Enterprises. When SOEs were created, a minimum of two shareholders was a legal requirement for companies. Although both "shareholding Ministers" have the same fiduciary rights and duties in relation to an SOE, a convention has evolved whereby each has a different policy focus. The Minister for SOEs is primarily concerned with an SOE's commercial performance, whereas the Minister of Finance is primarily concerned with an SOE's impact on the government's wider policy goals (*e.g.* relating to economic efficiency and fiscal policy). The roles of their advisers reflect these differences of focus.[3] SOE debt-holders also have an interest in SOE performance. All SOE debt instruments are required to include an acknowledgement that the debt is not government guaranteed.

2.4   SOE governance arrangements

Each SOE is formed as a company under the Companies Act 1993 and subject to its general provisions. In addition, each SOE must comply with specific governance and accountability provisions under the SOE Act 1986. The Act sets each SOE the primary goal of being "a successful business", and defines this as being as profitable as a comparable business not owned by the Crown, plus being a good employer and socially responsible. SOE voting shares may not be sold without Parliamentary approval. All SOEs are 100% government owned, with the voting shares held equally by two "shareholding Ministers" - the Minister of Finance and the "responsible Minister" (who by convention is normally the Minister for State Owned Enterprises).

The government's ownership relationship with an SOE (as spelt out in the SOE Act) can be viewed as a multi-period contract.[4] As with any company, the shareholders supply the SOE with equity capital. In return, they have the formal rights to appoint the SOE's directors, determine its constitution, and appropriate its residual earnings plus residual assets if the company is wound up. The Companies Act requires the directors of an SOE to act in good faith in what they believe to be in the best interests of the company.

The SOE Act requires each SOE board to provide the shareholding Ministers an annual Statement of Corporate Intent (SCI) setting the scope of business of the SOE, plus its broad goals and specific performance targets. The shareholding Ministers monitor the performance of the SOE and its board of directors. The Act also permits the shareholding Ministers to direct an SOE board to include particular items in the SCI, or omit them from it. Use of this power is subject to Parliamentary scrutiny, and may result in the shareholding Ministers being "deemed" to be directors under the Companies Act. Moreover, if the shareholding Ministers direct an SOE to provide goods or services that it normally would not provide as part of a commercial arrangement, the SOE can require the government to compensate it for any resultant financial detriment.

SOEs are taxed in the same way as privately-owned companies and are subject to the same set of commercial, safety and health regulations as other companies.

2.5   *Corporatisation and privatisation history*

Prior to the creation of SOEs, government-owned businesses in New Zealand were largely operated within various departments whose functions also included advising the government on policy issues.   This situation entailed frequent Ministerial involvement in their operations; multiple, sometimes unclear and often conflicting goals (*e.g.* employment creation versus profitability); and thus unclear accountability. Their transformation into SOEs yielded benefits from corporatisation - a clear commercial focus, and greatly improved accountability arrangements.   Since 1989 the government has privatised 13 SOEs for a total sale price of NZ$ 9.1 billion, in the context of 31 significant sales of government assets with a total sale price of NZ$ 15.9 billion.[5]

2.6   *Market and regulatory environment*

The government has sought to create an SOE only where it produces goods or services for which private markets operate or could operate - preferably with the prospect of competition or subject to a reasonably effective regulatory regime.   This approach recognises that market and regulatory arrangements have a vital impact on allocative as well as productive and dynamic efficiency.[6] Most of the existing SOEs do operate in markets which are already competitive or at least face the threat of competition.   The exceptions fall into two categories: natural[7] and statutory monopolies.

i)   *Natural monopolies*

The national electricity transmission grid, which Trans Power[8] owns and operates, is the only significant natural monopoly.[9] This SOE is subject to the generic regulatory regime - overseen by the Commerce Commission - which applies to all businesses operating in New Zealand.   The regime comprises three components:

>   −   *using the Commerce Act 1986* to deal with any alleged anti-competitive behaviour by the SOE, including the possibility of

court action being taken by private parties or the Commerce Commission;

- *extensive information disclosure* to make transparent the performance of the electricity industry businesses with market power (including Trans Power), to facilitate recourse to the provisions of the Commerce Act; and

- *the threat of applying further regulation*, such as price controls (which can be imposed under Part IV of the Commerce Act), if market dominance is abused.

As a consequence of this regulatory regime, and consistent with the government's overarching goal of economic efficiency, the board of Trans Power board has agreed with its shareholding Ministers (as part of its SCI) to set the SOE's prices such that over time its economic value remains constant. This commitment about the SOE's economic value is intended in effect to be a promise that the SOE will not exploit its monopoly position. It can be seen as consistent with the SOE's principal objective of being a successful business, and is intended partly to avoid any need for the government to impose explicit price controls on its activities.

ii)   Statutory monopolies

Two SOEs operate in markets where they have a statutory monopoly: NZ Post and the Airways Corporation. In NZ Post's case the monopoly's significance may be only transitory, due to the impact of technological changes. Its monopoly to deliver "basic letter post" is being steadily eroded by competition from substitutes stemming from continuing developments in communications technology. This competition was a major factor leading the SOE recently to lower its basic letter postal rate from the 45 cents maximum permitted level, to 40 cents, to protect its market share. The Airways Corporation - like Trans Power - has an agreement with its Shareholding Ministers to maintain over time a constant economic value.

3.   Nature of the issues

The shareholders of government-owned commercially-oriented companies (*i.e.* SOEs), like their private sector counterparts, generally face some problems in ensuring that companies operate in the most efficient manner. Conflicting interests of a company's board and management vis-à-vis the shareholders, create a motive for opportunistic behaviour by these agents of the shareholders. Monitoring difficulties for shareholders - stemming from the separation of ownership and control under the company model - may create scope for boards and management to act opportunistically to advance their own interests, rather than the best interests of the company and its shareholders.

The detrimental effect on efficiency can be more severe in the case of government-owned businesses, as the government faces some additional "agency problems" in ensuring that its commercial businesses operate efficiently. These problems include:

- weak external pressures from capital markets (for example, no threat of takeover), and often from product markets; and

- the political reasoning that produced public ownership often conflicts with economic efficiency.[10]

Privately owned companies, in contrast, do not experience these two latter problems and generally benefit from the effect that capital market pressures have in moderating the motive and scope for opportunism by boards and management.[11]

Key factors causing this state of affairs are discussed in more detail in the remainder of this section.[12]

3.1   *Insufficient market-related disciplines*

The boards and management of SOEs generally do not face significant capital market-related pressures that would encourage them to keep the total unit costs of their final products as low as possible. This is due to a combination of factors.

- *No threat of takeover of control:* The absence of any threat of a takeover removes a strong incentive for the board and management of an SOE to maximise its value. By contrast, a company with tradeable shares faces strong incentives to perform. The more closely it performs to its potential, the less the risk of the board and management losing their jobs as a result of a takeover.

- *Under-priced capital:* SOEs generally do not face the full opportunity cost of their equity capital - as their target rates of return are typically not expressed in relation to the market value of their assets. SOEs' equity capital is not continually marked to market values via share trading activity (unlike listed companies), nor usually subject to regular periodic revaluations to market value. Historic cost valuations are common. Even a mediocre return (relative to the market value of equity) can look reasonable when expressed as a rate of return on assets valued on a historic cost basis. As a result, SOEs do not have the same pressure to perform as their private sector counterparts. Also, they may be tempted to undertake projects that are not justifiable if allowance is made for the full opportunity cost of capital (*e.g.* electric power stations built earlier than needed).

— *Weak debt-holder monitoring:* Private debt holders have weak incentives to monitor SOE performance, to the extent they consider SOEs to be implicitly government guaranteed. Although all SOE debt instruments are required to include an acknowledgement that the debt is not guaranteed by the government, this disclaimer generally seems not to be believed. The financial markets have seen little evidence of a New Zealand government being prepared to let any such Crown-owned company fail financially and rely on its limited liability to restrict the Crown's financial exposure.

3.2   *Political economy of government ownership*

Government ownership of companies typically involves a number of features that tend to limit the relative economic efficiency of the companies.[13]

i)   *Electoral considerations*

The actions of government Ministers are quite naturally driven by a wide range of considerations that reflect the political basis of their roles. Political, social economic and commercial goals, for example, may need to be weighed against each other and trade-offs made between them where they conflict. Ultimately politicians are accountable to their electors and, therefore, bound to take note of their concerns. This accountability places real ongoing pressures on SOE shareholding Ministers not to lose sight of these concerns, even if it may mean trading off the extent to which an economic efficiency or commercial policy goal can be achieved. In summary, equity-holders of SOEs can be expected to find it difficult to focus single-mindedly on commercial or economic goals in managing their relationship with SOE boards.

ii)   No personal equity stake

The shareholding Ministers (and their advisers) have no personal equity stake in SOEs. Compared with major shareholders of private sector companies, therefore, they do not have strong personal financial incentives to monitor company performance closely, or otherwise to exercise formal shareholder rights to ensure the companies operate as efficiently as possible. In addition, New Zealand citizens - for whose collective benefit shareholding Ministers hold the shares - are poorly placed to monitor the companies. Individual citizens are unlikely to do so, for example, since they would bear all the costs but share any benefits with citizens collectively.[14]

iii)   Less certainty and credibility about business policy commitments

When the shareholders of an SOE commit to a particular set of business policy parameters governing its operations - as opposed to entering into a legally binding contract - the commitment is likely to be seen as less certain than if such a commitment were issued by private sector shareholders. This conclusion may be deduced from comparing aspects of private versus government ownership of businesses.

–   Private shareholders tend to be focused on a single clear goal (value maximisation), which may ensure a more stable and predictable approach than possible with government ownership. Capital market disciplines, including the threat of takeover[15], reinforce this focus by private sector shareholders.

Government shareholders' business policy decisions, however, may be influenced by multiple goals, changes of government[16] and changes in electoral factors within an executive electoral term.[17] Predicting how such factors are likely to impact on SOE related policies is more complex and, therefore, more difficult than with private sector ownership. Also, a government today cannot bind a future government's actions, which reduces the value of commitments.

Business policy commitments of private sector shareholders, therefore, are likely to be perceived as more certain and credible than those made by the shareholders of government owned entities.

41

iv)   *Unclear government intentions and expectations*

Unclear government intentions and expectations - particularly as regards the scale and scope of a business - increase the difficulty of holding an SOE board accountable for its role in the firm's performance. Unless at the outset the Shareholding Ministers make clear their preferences for the direction of the business, including its scale and scope, then the directors may not know where they stand in relation to expansion and diversification opportunities. This is likely to induce at least two sources of extra costs: renegotiation costs, and costs associated with making decisions contrary to the shareholders' expressed preferences or expectations. In either case, the outcome may not be economically efficient.

4.   Policies for enhancing economic efficiency

For those SOEs that the Government decides should remain Crown-owned in the longer term, shareholding Ministers can initiate a variety of measures that may improve the businesses' contribution to economic efficiency. This focus is broader than private shareholders usually take, since it is not limited solely to maximising the firm's value. While maximising profitability will generally result in SOEs being most efficient, this is not always so. In some cases, more efficient economic activity may result in the wider economy if an SOE forgoes some value-adding opportunities which are taken up instead by private investors.

This section discusses possible options for enhancing economic efficiency. It accepts value maximisation through time as a proxy test for achieving both productive and dynamic efficiency, and as consistent with allocative efficiency where an SOE's product market is either subject to significant competition, or an effective regulatory regime.

Applying an economic efficiency approach would still require SOEs to meet the principal goal of maximising value, but subject to any constraints imposed by the above emphasis on economic efficiency. Possible measures to implement this approach are outlined below. They fall into three main groups:

–   focusing on core activities

–   strengthening financial disciplines; and

- managing the on-going relationship between the government and the SOE.

4.1   Focusing on core activities

i)   Reducing scale and scope

Where Crown ownership of SOEs is to be retained, policy should be designed to ensure that these businesses operate as efficiently as possible and to ensure that the contribution of the SOE sector to economic efficiency is maximised. This can be achieved, in part, by:

- not extending its scope beyond a clearly defined set of core business activities or scale of operation (*e.g.* by declining proposed expansions, even though the expected return may exceed the cost of extra capital required);

- divesting assets that are not critical to the business; and

- limiting the level of equity to constrain the company's ability to broaden its scope or scale.

This constraint may impose opportunity costs on SOEs, by preventing them from undertaking value-adding projects that could take advantage of economies of scale or scope. It is not likely to impose costs on the wider economy, however, provided that other firms can undertake these projects at the same, or lesser incremental cost.[18] Other firms could be expected to do so, except where an SOE holds a unique set of assets or capabilities relevant to the project.[19]

Such uniqueness is most likely to exist where an SOE has a natural monopoly - such as Trans Power, and to a lesser extent Airways Corporation.[20] In other cases, as the market is able to sustain more than one supplier, other suppliers are likely to have similar assets and capabilities to the SOE, and therefore can be expected to be able to access similar economies of scale or scope.

Where an SOE has a unique set of assets or capabilities, any constraint on its scale or scope may impose costs on the wider economy (if other firms incur greater economic costs than the SOE would in undertaking the project). It may be possible to mitigate these costs by the SOE providing other firms access to the unique assets or capabilities it holds (*e.g.*, through franchising, leasing, or some other access agreement) providing the SOE access to a new set of incentives to seek higher performance. Where such access to other firms is not technically or commercially feasible, it may be efficient to relax the constraint on the SOE.

This feasibility, and the relative incremental costs faced by SOEs and privately owned firms to undertake a particular project, are likely to be difficult in practice to verify precisely. The government therefore may need to exercise a degree of judgement as to the situations in which it is efficient to relax the constraint. Alternatively, the government may employ general rules that on average are expected to yield the most efficient solution. An example would be to support an SOE's proposal to expand or diversify only where the SOE provides compelling reasons as to why it would face significantly lower incremental costs in undertaking the project, relative to other firms.

This focus on core activities has some important implications.

–   First, it may result in SOEs not undertaking value-adding projects otherwise available to them. The expectation is that private investors will undertake these projects.

–   Second, it means that through time the total value of an SOE business may intentionally be less than otherwise, and even decrease through time. This could occur, for example, if an SOE does not expand its core business, sheds non-core activities, and returns its excess capital to shareholders. In the government's balance sheet some of this value decrease would be offset by an increase in financial assets, reflecting the return of capital to shareholders.[21]

–   Third, it is likely to mean that the type of skills for directing and managing an SOE may change - with a requirement for people skilled in generating maximum value from a company that is not expanding.[22]

–   Fourth, where an SOE is a dominant player in its product markets, the fact that it will be constrained in terms of future expansion or diversification (and this is publicly known) may lower barriers to entry for potential competitors.[23] Lower barriers would result from the constraint on scope and scale reducing the extent to which an SOE could engage in deterrent behaviour.

The SOE Act provides mechanisms for the shareholding Ministers to influence the size and scope of an SOE's business - notably the Statement of Corporate Intent (SCI) that must be negotiated each year between an SOE board and the shareholders.[24] If agreement is not reached on issues to be covered in the SCI, the Act empowers the shareholding Ministers to direct the board to take the action sought.

ii)   *Operating structure changes*

A second means of focusing an SOE on its core value-adding activities is to consider whether alternative ways of structuring its operating arrangements would be likely to enhance shareholder value. The key boundary here is that between relying on the SOE's internal governance rules for decision making and contract enforcement, and relying on external market mechanisms. Options include: management contracting, franchising, contracting out, and leasing out. These options have the effect of altering the boundary of the company, and can be viewed as divesting, or withdrawing from various parts of the value chain of a business. In the extreme an SOE could become a shell (or virtual) company, with its primary function being the management of a set of contracts.

The following are operating structure options that could be considered in relation to each SOE's circumstances to improve the SOE's contribution to economic efficiency.[25]

- *Management contracting:* This option entails hiring an outside firm to manage some discrete part of a company's operations or to exercise operational control over the entire operations. It would mean devolving some rights to the contractor in return for various benefits such as access to specialist competencies and enabling the company to focus on its core business.

- *Franchising:* This option involves leasing out the right to use a clearly identifiable 'brand name' or other intellectual property owned by the SOE. This enhances unit manager's incentives to control costs as they have a direct stake in its profits.

- *Contracting out:* This means buying some of the goods and services needed to produce finished goods from an outside company. The benefits come from competitive-market pressures.

- *Leasing out:* This option entails transferring some of the rights of ownership to a lessee for a specified period. It could be used when the government is willing to devolve control of a portion of a business into the hands of someone who can operate it more efficiently.

These options may improve efficiency in one or more of the following ways:

- by shifting some responsibility outside the company, as a means of overcoming the limitations of hierarchical SOE governance arrangements;

- by harnessing the benefits of competitive markets for intermediate products or services; and/or

- benefiting from stronger incentives to produce at least cost, by shifting some control to parties that typically have stronger incentives to minimise costs.

The foregoing options are matters within the ambit of each SOE board's responsibilities. We consider that shareholding Ministers should urge each SOE board to evaluate the possibility of achieving efficiency gains from one or more of the above operating options where they are feasible. This is consistent with shareholding Ministers adopting a more active monitoring role.

4.2   Strengthening financial disciplines

The capital structure of a company determines the nature of the claims on a company's cash flows, and the company's financial flexibility.[26] Debt financing typically commits the company to specified servicing costs (in cash), whereas equity financing provides the company with greater financial discretion. Empirical evidence suggests there is a broad range of debt: equity ratios over which a particular company's cost of capital is minimised, allowing some latitude in the mix of debt and equity without significantly altering its overall cost of capital.

A degree of financial flexibility is necessary to enable a company to accommodate down-side deviations from its business plan without major disruption to its operations or undermining its market position. However excess flexibility can be costly, to the extent that it:

- reduces external discipline on managers to control costs;

- increases the likelihood that management will invest in projects that do not at least return their cost of capital, that is projects which erode company value; and

- signals to potential new entrants the possibility for the SOE to engage in deterrent behaviour.

Most SOEs typically have had relatively large free cash flows after meeting all costs, including debt obligations, but before paying dividends. These free cash flows are the primary source used by SOEs to expand, and they also reduce the discipline on management to maintain and enhance company value.[27]

Reducing the level of these free cash flows by paying them out to the suppliers of capital could be achieved in two ways: substituting private[28] debt for government equity; and/or raising dividend levels. This would strengthen financial disciplines on an SOE, and can be expected to enhance productive efficiency.

- *Substituting private debt for equity* would raise the requirement on SOEs to meet their capital costs in cash, and thereby reduce the cash pool available for use at the discretion of a board. This would place greater discipline on managers to control costs and only take on those projects which return at least their cost of capital. It may also strengthen the incentives on the debt holders to monitor the SOEs,[29] and free up government capital for other uses.

- *Raising dividend levels* would similarly raise the requirement on SOEs to meet their capital costs in cash, but would not free up government capital as quickly.

Where an SOE is a dominant player in its product markets, strengthening its financial disciplines is also likely to reduce barriers to entry of potential competitors into these or related areas of business activity. Lower entry barriers would result from the SOE having less financial capacity to deter entry into its product markets. Without such change, potential entrants may be deterred on account of viewing the SOE as an aggressive party, with relatively lower profit expectations from its owners. This concern parallels the "deep pockets" situation referred to in the industrial organisation literature.[30]

The shareholding Ministers' ability to influence an SOE's capital structure is basically via the SCI negotiation process.

4.3   Managing the Government - SOE relationship

Continued government ownership of SOEs raises the issue of how the relationship between government and the SOE should be managed through time. In New Zealand this relationship is prescribed in broad terms by the State Owned Enterprises Act 1986 - this section explores various aspects of the relationship within that context.

i)   Clarifying and communicating the government's intentions

At present SOEs and the shareholding Ministers (and their advisers) tend to debate issues about the capital structure and scope of an SOE's business on a case by case basis. The focus of such debates is usually on implications for the SOE's value. Discussion of the issues, and any ensuing decisions, would be better informed if the shareholding Ministers both articulated their preferences and expectations more clearly (taking into account broader economic concerns), and communicated them to the interested parties. A public commitment to clearly stated expectations would enhance the credibility of such expectations by raising the cost to the shareholders of deviating from them. A possible means for achieving this would be for the shareholders to issue a statement of shareholder expectations (SSE). Such a statement would apply to SOE policy some of the principles already adopted in relation to fiscal policy through the Fiscal Responsibility Act.[31]

If the shareholding Ministers signal that each SOE should focus on its core activities and reduce its free cash flows, it will be important for them to communicate clearly that the value of the government's equity in the SOE may decrease over time. This would encourage SOE management to concentrate on the task at hand, rather than seeking out value-adding projects in related (but not core) areas of business. The extra costs incurred by shareholding Ministers in preparing and promulgating an SSE would lower the degree of renegotiations later with the Board and correspondingly lower renegotiation costs. This would be especially true where an SOE had already incurred costs investing in specific assets that later turned out to be inconsistent with the shareholders' expectations for the business. [32]

An important aspect of the proposed SSE is to avoid potential market entrants having to second guess the government about the future scope and scale of an SOE. This would increase the certainty for private investors and thereby encourage them to enter the market and compete.

In summary, the greater certainty provided both to SOE management and to private sector entrants should reduce the costs associated with incomplete contracting problems.

ii)   *Monitoring and value-based reporting*

The relative lack of capital-market related pressure on SOEs means that the shareholding Ministers need to rely on administrative monitoring procedures to hold SOE boards accountable. Current practice includes setting expected financial performance targets in the SCI for the future three years, and reporting against those targets at quarterly, half yearly and full year intervals. Boards are required to explain significant deviations from expected financial performance targets. In addition, each SOE may be subject to a business review at periodic intervals, normally no more frequent than five yearly. Such monitoring provides a basis for the shareholding Ministers to consider the future direction of the company, and any changes that may be required.

This monitoring is basically reactive and focused on published ex post financial performance measures.

As SOEs do not face the capital market mechanisms that help to align the interests of private sector shareholders and their agents (boards and management)[33], a more proactive approach to monitoring would seem justified.[34] This would comprise more extensive exercise of the shareholders' formal rights to exercise residual control. In particular, shareholding Ministers could become more involved in the process of setting the strategic direction of each SOE, but not intervening in operational decisions required to implement the strategy. The aim is to provide clear goals for SOE boards to achieve and strengthen the incentives for them to do so - with the underlying goal of maximising SOEs' contribution to economic efficiency.

The general adoption of value-based reporting (VBR) by SOEs would enhance shareholding Ministers' ability to assess the extent to which an SOE is creating or eroding value. VBR involves a company reporting its economic returns, the opportunity cost of the capital used to produce these returns, and the extent to which its various activities add to or reduce its value.[35]

VBR, therefore, is a very useful tool that the shareholding Ministers could use both to set performance targets and to measure performance against them objectively. VBR could place an extra discipline on the way investment proposals are evaluated, by more clearly identifying the extent to which proposals are likely to add value. VBR also could be an effective basis for boards to develop performance-based remuneration structures to encourage managers to maximise value. For all these reasons, SOEs' adoption of VBR would facilitate improvements in their productive and dynamic efficiency.

iii)   *Director appointments and performance*

An SOE's board of directors has a crucial role in maintaining and improving the company's performance. From the government's viewpoint, therefore, it is important both to obtain sufficient suitably-skilled directors to oversee these companies, and to ensure that each board of directors has strong incentives to enhance a company's value. The following are some key measures that could help the government to secure the best performance from its SOE directors.

- *Introducing more independence and objectivity into the selection process:* Selecting SOE directors on the basis of more systematically matching candidates' skills and experience to meet a particular set of job specifications tailored (as necessary) for a particular SOE.

- *More clearly specifying the equity holders' expectations of directors:* This could be achieved by the equity holders providing clear terms of reference for individual directors when they are appointed, and each board as a whole via the proposed SSE.

- *Strengthening directors' incentives to ensure the company performs well:* Directors' incentives could be strengthened by introducing performance-related rewards and sanctions, and enhancing accountability mechanisms (including shareholder monitoring of the SOE, and value-based reporting).

5.   Conclusions

In New Zealand a significant number of SOEs have now been privatised. For those SOE businesses that remain government owned, an important issue is how best to govern them, given the weaker incentives to operate efficiently inherent in this form of ownership. This paper has outlined a set of measures that, if adopted, would both limit exposure to the problem of these weaker incentives, and strengthen incentives for SOEs to perform where the exposure remains.

The essence of these measures include:

– focusing the SOEs on their core activities, with an expected reduction in their scale and scope. This could include focusing an SOE on particular markets, and also adopting operating structures that change the boundaries of the firm. The key boundary here is between relying on the SOE's internal governance rules for decision making and contract enforcement, as compared with relying on external market mechanisms;

– strengthening financial disciplines on SOEs by withdrawing more of their free cash flows, through substituting debt for equity, and raising dividend levels; and

– strengthening the management of the government - SOE relationship by clarifying and communicating the government's intentions for these businesses, ensuring a well structured director appointment and assessment process, introducing value based reporting, and bolstering other monitoring processes.

While much of the case for these measures is based on theoretical argument, it is important to test the ideas empirically. We see this as an important area for further research.

Appendix I

SUMMARY FINANCIAL DATA AS AT 30 JUNE 1996
(For SOEs trading in December 1996)

State-Owned Enterprise	Annual revenue $m	Operating surplus $m	Total assets (book value) $m	Equity (book value) $m	Percentage of total equity Cum.	
					%	%
ECNZ[a]	1 383	322	3535	2066	35.9	35.9
Trans Power	542	95	31 100	1361	23.7	59.6
Contact Energy	210	40	1401	928	16.1	75.7
Land Corp	71	29	513	441	7.7	83.4
NZ Post	655	71	499	265	4.6	88.0
TVNZ	442	50	492	241	4.2	92.2
Govt. Property Services	32	3	289	161	2.8	95.0
Timberlands West Coast	27	10	129	122	2.1	97.1
CoalCorp	192	17	178	105	1.8	98.9
Airways Corporation	91	1	171	46	0.8	99.7
Met Service	23	3	13	10	0.2	99.9
Vehicle Testing NZ	18	1	12	5	0.1	100.0
Total[b]	3 686	642	10 342	57 515751	100	100

Notes:

a   Contact Energy took over eight power stations from The Electricity Corporation of New Zealand (ECNZ) on 1 February 1996, to form a second major electricity generating company in New Zealand. In this table ECNZ's revenue and operating surplus for 1994/95 are allocated to the two companies on the basis of market share at 1 February 1996. Total assets and equity are allocated according to Contact Energy's opening financial position, with the residual allocated to ECNZ.

b   This table omits Crown Forestry Management Limited, and NZ Railways Corporation, both of which own few assets and are not operating companies. The table also omits Terralink, as this SOE did not commence trading until 1 July 1997.

Source: Authors.

PARTIAL SALE AS A MEANS TO ENHANCE EFFICIENCY

The paper has focused on the government either being the only equity holder in any SOE, or divesting all its shares. Interim positions are possible. A partial sale (including new issues) would result in an additional party(s) holding an equity contract with the company. Private owners[36] can be expected to place greater pressure on the company to enhance its value than if it remained wholly government owned. Some private owners may also bring additional expertise to the company.

Any extra discipline and expertise that partial private ownership may bring to bear on an SOE's operations, however, are likely to have a significant effect only where:

–   *Private owners hold a sufficiently large parcel to warrant them incurring monitoring costs.* The more concentrated the shareholding, the stronger the incentives will be for private owners to monitor the company. Any transfer of expertise would be dependent on the identity of the shareholder.

–   *SOE directors place more weight on the preferences of the private sector shareholders relative to those of the government shareholders.* This implies the board would discount any wider public policy concerns of the government shareholders, where these conflicted with action to maximise the company's value.

The potential advantages need to be weighed against a number of disadvantages, including the following.

–   If a partial sale of an SOE led to listing of its shares, stringent legislative controls on insider-trading would apply to the company. If private ownership of the shares is widely disbursed, the practical effect may be to constrain significantly the company's ability to inform the government about commercially sensitive aspects of the company's performance. Any such constraints on information flows to the major shareholders (including the government), would reduce their ability to monitor the company's performance. This impact would need to be weighed against the benefits of other monitoring as a result of listing. These benefits from listing are likely to be less than generally received, however, due to the involvement of the government as a large shareholder.

— Other shareholders may be successful in accessing the "deep pockets" of the government to increase the value of their shares, particularly in times of financial distress[37]. This perception can be expected to lower their incentive to monitor the performance of the company.

Although introducing some private equity into an SOE may enhance economic efficiency, the resultant governance structure is likely to be less effective than would be the case if all the equity were transferred to the private sector.

NOTES

1.   This is elaborated in Skilling (1996a).

2.   Appendix I provides summary financial data on the fifteen SOEs.

3.   The Crown Company Monitoring and Advisory Unit (CCMAU) is the principal adviser to the Minister for SOEs, and the Treasury is the principal adviser to the Minister of Finance.

4.   Jensen and Meckling (1976), Fama and Jensen (1983) and Hansmann (1988, 1996), provide insightful analysis of various ownership structures and their economic implications.

5.   These figures are as at 31 December 1996.

6.   This approach is consistent with the analysis of Vickers and Yarrow (1988).

7.   A "natural monopoly" exists where output costs in a market for a particular product or its close substitutes are minimised by having only one supplier.

8.   Trans Power accounts for about 18% of the government's equity in SOEs.

9.   The Airways Corporation also has a natural monopoly in some of its markets, but changes in technology are reducing the extent of this natural monopoly.

10.   Mueller (1993), especially chapters 9, 13, 14 and 17 thoroughly analyses the impacts of political economy factors.

11.   Megginson et al (1994) found strong performance improvement from privatisation in a study of 61 privatised companies in 18 countries. Vining and Boardman (1992) found privately owned firms tend to out-perform their state-owned counterparts. Galal et al (1995) showed that in a sample of 12 privatisations in four countries, that net welfare increased in 11 of the cases. Domberger and Piggott (1994) argue that "the case for privatisation rests on the incentives and constraints that the market provides to promote

55

[productive] efficiency within the firm." They found the empirical evidence, however, provided inconclusive support for privatisation. A World Bank report (1995) found that the gains from privatisation and other related reforms are substantial, although only a few countries have reformed their SOEs successfully. Vickers and Yarrow (1991) emphasise that the effects of privatisation in any particular context will depend significantly on the wider market, regulatory and institutional environments in which it is implemented.

12.   See Brumby, Hyndman and Jamie (1996) for further details.

13.   Moe (1991) and Horn (1995) highlight the implications of political economy issues for the structure and operation of government entities.

14.   These logistical and "free-rider" problems have been discussed in the literature by various authors, including Hart (1995) p.127, and Mueller (1989).

15.   Which also provides a mechanism for shareholders to exit the company.

16.   Shareholding Ministers and their SOE policies may change whenever the political party, or coalition, holding executive government power changes. Control of executive government is contested at least every three years.

17.   Moe (1991) and Horn (1995) discuss how political institutions are designed partly for performance and partly for protection against political uncertainty, but often at a cost to the performance goals.

18.   This approach, which focuses on incremental costs, assumes SOEs and privately owned firms face the same conditions in other dimensions of the project (eg the same output prices). In practice market conditions are likely to change through time, which raises dynamic efficiency concerns as to the relative abilities of different firms to adapt and take advantage of new opportunities. It seems reasonable to expect privately owned firms will be at least as efficient in a dynamic sense as an SOE, as they are likely to have stronger incentives to adapt.

19.   Uniqueness in this case refers to any assets or capabilities that the SOE holds that provide it with a significant comparative advantage in relation to the particular project.

20.   It may also arise in the case of a statutory monopoly, such as in the case of NZ Post, as a result of economic distortions created by the statutory constraint.

21.   The clarity of this accounting outcome requires the government to compile and report a government sector balance sheet.

22.   A key assumption in this approach is the availability of directors and managers that are capable and willing to work to this objective.

23.   The investment constraints placed on ECNZ subsequent to the formation of Contact Energy are an example of this.

24.   See Section 2.4 above.

25.   The nature, implications and suitability conditions for each option that is discussed in this section are analysed in generic terms by Brumby, Hyndman and Jamie (1996), pp 34-58.

26.   Financial flexibility refers to the ability to meet obligations at short notice and reasonable cost under a range of financial market circumstances.

27.   Jensen (1986) outlines agency issues associated with a company's free cash flows and the use of debt as one means of addressing these issues.

28.   Private debt is recommended as the Government does not appear to have a comparative advantage in supplying debt capital to SOEs. It would also increase the SOE's potential exposure to another source of monitoring and potential pressure to perform efficiently.

29.   Any strengthening would depend on debt holders having some concern that the Government would not meet all their costs in the event of financial distress, ie that any implicit Government guarantee was not complete.

30.   Dasgupta and Stiglitz (1987), for example, discuss the relationship between potential and actual competition where even a small degree of sunk costs are involved.

31.   For an explanation of this legislation see New Zealand Treasury (1996). The Act sets out to achieve the following: (i) to increase the transparency of policy intentions and the economic and fiscal consequences of policy; (ii) to bring a long-term focus to budgeting; (iii) to disclose the aggregate impact of the budget prior to the detailed annual allocations; (iv) to ensure independent assessment and reporting of fiscal policy; and (v) to facilitate parliamentary and public scrutiny of economic and fiscal information and plans (p.7).

32.   See Hart (1993) and Aghion & Bolton (1992) for a discussion of incomplete contracting issues.

33.   Takeovers are not possible, and shareholders cannot sell their voting shareholding without Parliamentary approval.

34.   This approach is advocated by Skilling (1996b).

35.   See Rappaport (1986) and Stewart (1991) for a comprehensive explanation of VBR.

36.   With their associated capital-market disciplines.

37.   The Bank of New Zealand is an example. On sale of the BNZ to the National Australia Bank in 1992, the Government and one other large shareholder provided guarantees for a range of contingent liabilities, with small shareholders providing no such guarantees but nevertheless receiving the same price for their shares.

REFERENCES

AGHION Philippe and BOLTON Patrick, "An Incomplete Contracts Approach to Financial Contracting", *Review of Economic Studies*, Vol. 59, 1992, pp. 473-494.

BRUMBY Jim, HYNDMAN Michael, and JAMIE John, *Crown Company Structure Options*, unpublished New Zealand Treasury staff working paper, June 1996.

DASGUPTA Partha, and STIGLITZ Joseph E., *Potential Competition, Actual Competition, and Economic Welfare*, Discussion Paper 8, Department of Economics, Woodrow Wilson School of Public and International Affairs, Princeton University, August 1987.

DOMBERGER Simon, and PIGGOTT John, "Privatisation Policies and Public Enterprise: A Survey", in *Privatisation and Economic Performance* ed. Matthew Bishop, John Kay and Colin Mayer; Oxford University Press, 1994.

FAMA Eugene and F JENSEN Michael C., "Separation of Ownership and Control", *Journal of Law and Economics,* Vol 26, June 1983; pp 327-349.

GALAL Ahmed, JONES Leroy, TANDON Pankaj, and VOGELSANG Ingo, *Welfare Consequences of Selling Public Enterprises: An Empirical Analysis*, 1994.

HANSMANN Henry, "Ownership of the Firm*", Journal of Law, Economics and Organization,* Vol 4, 1988; pp 267-304.

HANSMANN Henry, *The Ownership of Enterprise*, The Belknap Press of Harvard University Press, 1996.

HART Oliver, *Firms, Contracts and Financial Structure*, Clarendon Press, 1995.

HORN Murray J, *The Political Economy of Public Administration: Institutional Choice in the Public Sector,* Cambridge University Press, 1995.

JENSEN Michael C., "Agency Costs of Free Cash Flow, Corporate Finance, and Takeovers", *American Economic Review,* Vol 76, No 2, 1986; pp 323-329.

JENSEN Michael C, MECKLING William H, "Theory of the Firm: Managerial Behaviour, Agency Costs and Ownership Structure", *Journal of Financial Economics,* Vol 3, 1976; pp 305-360.

MEGGINSON, William L, NASH Robert C, and VAN RANDENBORGH Matthias, "The Financial and Operating Performance of Newly Privatised Firms: An International Empirical Analysis"; *Journal of Finance,* Vol XLIX, No. 2, 1994; pp. 403-452.

MOE, Terry M., "Politics and the Theory of Organisation", *Journal of Law, Economics and Organisation,* Vol 7, Special Issue, 1991; pp 106-129.

MUELLER Dennis C., *Public Choice II;* Cambridge University Press,1989.

NEW ZEALAND TREASURY, *Fiscal Responsibility Act 1994: An Explanation*, GP Print Limited, 1996.

RAPPAPORT Alfred, *Creating Shareholder Value: The New Standard for Business Performance,* Free Press, 1986.

ROMANO Roberta, "A Guide to Takeovers: Theory, Evidence and Regulation", *Yale Journal on Regulation,* Vol 9, No 1, 1992; pp 119-180.

SKILLING David, *A Framework for Governance of the Commercial Companies on the Crown Balance Sheet*, unpublished NZ Treasury staff working paper, May 1996. [a]

SKILLING David, *A Framework for Active Monitoring*; unpublished NZ Treasury staff working paper, December 1996. [b]

STEWART G Bennett, "The Quest for Value" *A Guide for Senior Managers, Harper Collins*, 1991.

VICKERS John and YARROW George, *Privatization: An Economic Analysis*; MIT Press, 1988.

VICKERS John and YARROW George, "Economic Perspectives on Privatisation, *Journal of Economic Perspectives*, Vol 5, No. 2, Spring 1991.

WEINGAST, Barry R., "Constitutions as Governance Structures: The Political Foundations of Secure Markets", *Journal of Institutional and Theoretical Economics*, Vol 149 (1), March 1993.

ZECKAUSER Richard J, and POUND John, "Are Large Shareholders Effective Monitors? An Investigation of Share Ownership and Corporate Performance", *Asymmetric Information, Corporate Finance and Investment*; ed. R. Glenn Hubbard, University of Chicago Press, 1990.

THE PRIVATISATION PROCESS AND CORPORATE GOVERNANCE: THE FRENCH CASE

by

François Morin[*]

The French experience of privatisation shows that, in many cases, there is far more involved than just a transfer of corporate ownership. Along with such transfers can come a change in management and even a radical restructuring of a firm's deliberative or executive authority. In this latter case, the change in ownership goes hand in hand with a shift in the manner of corporate governance.

But the process can go much farther than that and actually transform a company's strategic perspective: the introduction of extension cross-holdings between companies with common strategic interests can alter the state of market competition and affect the channels through which the economy is financed.

In both of the recent waves of privatisation in France - initially in 1986-88 (the first period of so-called "cohabitation" between a socialist executive and a conservative parliament centre) and subsequently in 1993-95 (the second such period), the Government opted for governance structures for firms which were to be privatised, known as "groups of stable shareholders".

The purpose of this paper is to explain the logic behind the introduction of stable shareholder groupings through a discussion of the Government's chosen method of privatisation (Part I), and, at the same time, to show how this choice affected corporate governance; Part II seeks to shed some light on the coeur financier ("financial heart") of the French economy.

---

*   Laboratoire d'Études et de Recherches en Économie de la Production (LEREP). Université de Toulouse I.

I. Method of privatisation and the emergence of stable shareholders

Theoretically, there were two competing approaches the Government could have taken in choosing a method of privatisation: an approach based on competitive bidding; or a strategic approach, in which existing (or potentially productive) ties with companies would result in the selection of specific investors.

The first approach -- competitive bidding -- clearly conforms to the financial market model, with investors primarily concerned with safety and profitability through a diversification of their security portfolios. The second approach -- strategic configuration -- involves the constitution of a "financial heart": here, the tender process tends to favour the firm's partners or allies in order to strengthen a communality of strategic interests[1].

The model chosen by the authorities in 1986 clearly reflected the second approach. To be sure, an appeal to the financial market remains an important component of the model, but one that takes second place to the Government's determination to ensure some degree of national control over the capital handed over to the private sector.

This determination was unflinching throughout the privatisation process, its most spectacular manifestation being the creation of groups of stable shareholders. In the most recent round of privatisation, this approach was taken even further with the transfer of publicly-held capital to reference shareholders.

From stable shareholders to "noyau dur" (or inner core)

There are a number of steps in a privatisation strategy centred on the constitution of a stable shareholder base. An inevitable outcome is to set up what the French call a *noyau dur*, or close-knit group of core shareholders, in the manner described below.

In the initial phase, the Government must first ensure that it has overall control over the privatisation. It generally does so by appointing a new Chairman, who will remain in place after privatisation. Politically, this new chief executive naturally has the Government's confidence.

The new Chairman is then expected to personally establish the necessary contacts with those who will ultimately become the stable shareholders of the privatised enterprise. Ties among these shareholders are in many cases reinforced by formal agreements; for example, "stability pacts" were signed in respect of all of the firms that were privatised in 1986 and 1987, except for Compagnie Générale d'Électricité (CGE). Such pacts generally stipulate a minimum holding period and give other signatories a right of first refusal if any shares are subsequently sold.

Once the firm is valued by the Privatisation Commission and the group of stable shareholders is approved by the Minister for Economic and Financial Affairs, the public offer of sale can proceed in a series of tranches. The first is reserved for this select group, another for institutional investors, a third for employees and a final tranche for the public at large.

When the sell-off is complete, a shareholders' meeting is called to elect the new board of directors. In turn, those directors appoint their chairman. It should be stressed that, for each of the firms privatised in France in this manner, the chairman-elect has been the one initially selected by the Government to carry out the process. Naturally, this last outcome is no accident. It is a direct consequence of the way in which all of these managers have gone about recruiting their stable shareholders. The following diagrams shed light on the approach to ownership that prevailed in each case.

Privatisation
and the group of stable shareholders

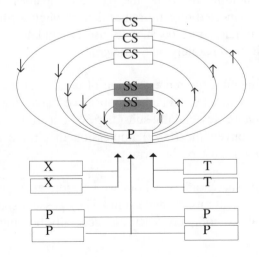

As is fairly clear from the diagram, the group of stable shareholders is not uniform. A distinction can be made between two sets of stable shareholders of the privatised parent company ("**P**"): shareholders in the closed core (*noyau bouclé*) and traditional shareholders.

Shareholders in the closed core are interconnected through loops of circular shareholdings. Legally, there are three types of circular shareholding in France: self-shareholding (*participations d'autocontrôle*), cross-shareholding (*participations croisées*) and reciprocal shareholding (*participations réciproques*):

- *Self-shareholding* refers to ownership of shares in a group by that group's own constituent elements, *i.e.* by subsidiaries (or other firms controlled by the parent company); one or more of these shareholdings involve shares in the parent company, and, as a result, the corresponding voting rights lie entirely in the hands of group management. In the diagram, such shareholdings are labelled **SS**.

- *Cross-shareholding* is also circular, but the loop includes a "friendly" group. It is therefore to the advantage of the two groups linked in this manner, and thus of their managers, that these shareholdings (and especially the voting rights attaching thereto) be administered in the best interests of the management teams in place. These shareholdings are labelled **CS**.

- *Reciprocal shareholding* refers to a particular type of cross-shareholding in which the parent companies of two groups are interconnected directly rather than through affiliates. In practice, this is fairly rare because its use is regulated. Such ties are not depicted separately on the diagram.

In our diagram, the representation of circular shareholdings has been simplified in the extreme. In the loops, we have naturally eliminated intermediate companies (essentially subsidiaries) so as to show significant links only. This may convey the (false) impression that these shareholdings are reciprocal in the legal sense of the term.

The other shareholders, whom we categorise as "traditional", reflect totally asymmetrical patterns of ownership. They possess significant blocks of shares in the privatised company (each one generally holding between 0.5 and

5 per cent of the equity), but the privatised company is not one of their own shareholders.

Shareholders can also be divided into a number of blocks, including:

- Public or semi-public shareholders -- or even the State -- labelled **T** in the diagram), which, with the permission of the competent authorities, may purchase some of the shares on offer. In most cases these shareholders were, in fact, already present prior to privatisation and have been asked by the State to retain an equity interest and thus not to sell off all of their shares. These shares are obviously extremely valuable to the incumbent management, because they afford it additional protection against potential raiders.

- Foreign shareholders (**X**), of which there were virtually none among the invited reference shareholders of the initial wave of privatisation. In this respect the situation began to change in 1993. Almost all of the foreign shareholders have been institutional investors.

- Other private shareholders (**P**), who are not in the closed core but who nonetheless agree, for reasons of their own, to acquire an equity interest. By design, these shareholders do not occupy the same strategic position as private shareholders in the inner core. Management does not have the same hold on them, because here the power relationship is asymmetrical.

This presentation of the two major groups of shareholders is obviously crucial to an understanding of the structure of corporate governance in privatised enterprises. In firms that are privatised by means of the stable shareholder method, a clear majority of the Board of Directors is always made up by representatives of the first group of shareholders, *i.e.* by representatives of the closed core.

Managers from within the corporate group are represented on these boards via self-shareholdings, while managers from other groups are also present, via cross-shareholdings. Together, these inside and outside directors constitute what we have called the "closed inner core" (*noyau dur bouclé*) and ensure that a majority of shareholders will vote in their favour at general meetings.

This composite, and to some extent circular, make-up neutralises the role of ownership: the managing technostructure secures power on which there is no real check. From its own viewpoint, this is probably the system's greatest advantage. And since the inner core, by definition, forms a loop, the practice gives rise to a communality of interest which transcends the enterprise and brings it into a network of strategic alliances.

Closed inner cores in privatised French companies

It is a well-known fact that most of the major privatisation in France has been carried out, since 1986, in accordance with this principle of a closed inner core of shareholders[2]. Part of the equity (generally between 25 and 45 per cent) is sold off to a limited number of investors who as a rule are industrial or financial partners of the privatised enterprise; together they form the circle of stable shareholders.

Among these stable shareholders, however, is a smaller, "strategic" group whose members agree to reciprocal share ownership. These closed inner cores hold significant interests of between 10 and 30 per cent of total equity and generally constitute between one- and two-thirds of the stable shareholder base.

However, the composition of these groups of core investors shifted between 1986 and 1993. A 1989 legislative reform of self-shareholding, which entered into force on 1 July 1991, stripped the practice of much of its appeal. In contrast, and probably as a substitute, cross-shareholdings became more widespread and since 1993 have constituted the financial backbone of the core.

The period of less than one year between December 1986 and October 1987 saw the most extensive privatisation of the French economy. Among the sell-offs were the financial corporations Suez, Paribas, Société Générale and CCF, but also Saint-Gobain, Compagnie Générale d'Électricité, Havas and so on.

By way of illustration, below is a description of how three of these firms were privatised, and how their stable cores were structured. In May 1988, a few months after privatisation:

- Paribas had 14 stable shareholders, together possessing 31 per cent of the equity; there were no foreign investors among the shareholders; public shareholdings still accounted for nearly 10 per cent of total equity. The closed inner core consisted of five investors with an aggregate interest of 13 per cent; among them was Compagnie Bancaire, whose 6.7 per cent stake was the greatest instance of self-shareholding.

– Suez had a roughly equivalent shareholder structure: the stable core (15 shareholders) held a total of about 38 per cent of the equity, with no foreign investors and a significant (17.5 per cent) share of public ownership. The closed inner core held a 10.5 per cent stake split among five members, three of whom -- together owning 5.5 per cent -- represented self-shareholding.

– CGE had only nine stable shareholders, who together owned 25.5 per cent of the equity. Among them was a Swiss investor and a lone public company (slated for privatisation). In contrast, the closed core was slightly more extensive than in the two previous examples, with a 13.4 per cent interest divided among four shareholders, with self-shareholding via Compagnie Immobilière Méridionale.

Above we have described the standard method of privatisation during France's first period of "cohabitation". For the most part, privatisation subsequent to March 1993 followed the same pattern.

However, the Privatisation Act of 19 July 1993 gave the Privatisation Commission new powers over the selection of stable-core shareholders, while allowing the Minister for Economic Affairs considerable discretion.

The first noteworthy change was that the constitution of stable cores was no longer mandatory. The Act stipulating that "the Minister with responsibility for the economy may decide to call upon non-market buyers". Secondly, the Act gave the Privatisation Commission a say in the choice of investors; as for the Minister, he could issue decrees only if based on a favourable opinion of the Commission. Let it be recalled that in 1986 there had been criticism from all quarters denouncing the Minister's predominant role in forging stable groups of shareholders.

Privatisation of Paribas
and the Group of Stable Shareholders
May 1988

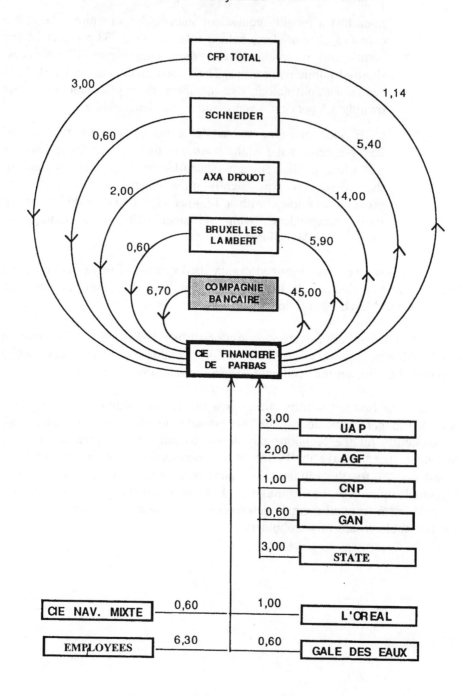

Privatisation of Suez
and the Group of Stable Shareholders
May 1988

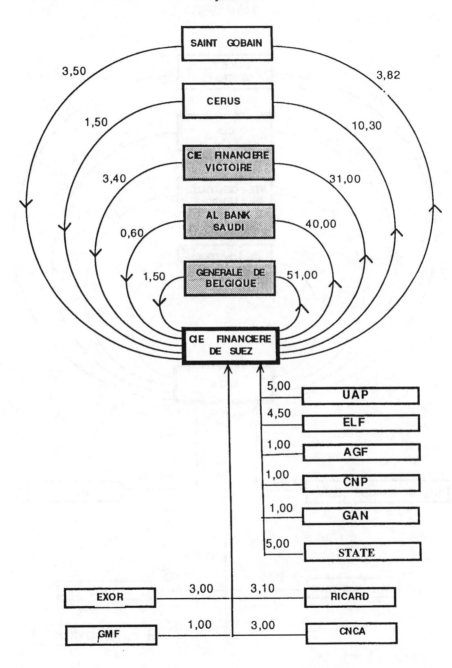

Privatisation of CGE
(subsequently Alcatel)
and the Group of Stable Shareholders
May 1988

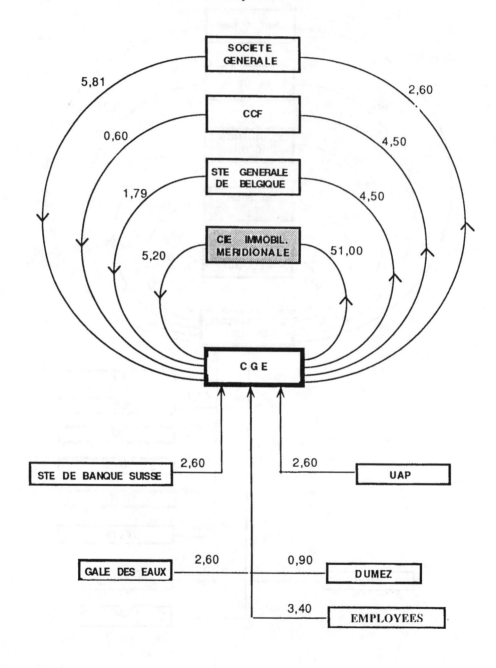

The announcement by the Minister for Economic Affairs on 4 October 1993, regarding the composition of the stable core of shareholders for Banque Nationale de Paris (BNP), was illuminating in quite a number of respects; for one, the group included the bank's major clients and partners, along with its main allies, among them Dresdner Bank and (especially) Union des Assurances de Paris (UAP). These choices alone clearly reflected a bank/industry perspective, but that perspective can be further confirmed by a closer look at the ownership structure, and at the cross-shareholdings in particular (see chart of BNP shareholders).

The stable shareholders were to consist of 16 investors who between them would hold nearly 48 per cent of the equity. This impressive proportion was never actually reached, since in the end Dresdner Bank did not acquire its announced 10 per cent share, but only 1 per cent. Here, for the first time, foreign investors played an integral part in the privatisation, five such partners having been approached. For its part, the announced inner core was particularly imposing, at nearly 30 per cent (actually 21 per cent, in view of Dresdner's defection).

But the most symptomatic feature is probably the absence of self-shareholding. All of the circular shareholdings in this case are cross-shareholdings. This can be explained, as mentioned earlier, by the legislation in force since 1 July 1991 which strips self-held shares of their voting rights. Such shareholding is not against the law (it still exists), but these particular shares no longer carry any votes. This has triggered massive use of cross-shareholding, which is in no way regulated and yet produces perfectly genuine voting rights.

The BNP example (and also those of firms privatised thereafter) offers clear confirmation of the approach underlying the systems of corporate governance that were put in place. Their basic purpose is to entrench management's power as solidly as possible. Nevertheless, the legitimacy of this power is neither self-evident nor indisputable, since the equity on which the power is based, being a closed loop, is largely fictitious. Lastly, the ties thus created produce very real effects, since they expand the strategic horizons of the groups concerned. *By construction, the inner cores are in fact closed loops.* This practice therefore engenders a communality of interests wider than that of the enterprise alone.

Privatisation of BNP
and the Group of Stable Shareholders
October 1993

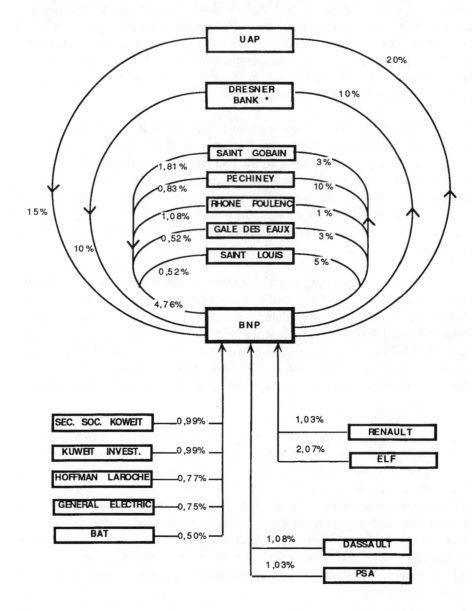

* Here we indicate cross-shareholdings as they had been negotiated prior to privatisation; under the agreement between the two groups, effective implementation was to take place after privatisation had been fully completed.

II.   Corporate governance and the French "coeur financier" or financial heart

The networks created by the closed inner cores have the particularity of a relatively stable make-up. They form industrial and financial complexes whose action often spans a number of years[3]. These complexes therefore constitute networks of intergroup alliances, each of which has its own identity, incorporates a vast variety of activities and lines of business and, in most instances, develops strategic interactions with others within the same sphere of operations: the financial heart[4].

Below is a brief retrospective on the formation of strategic alliances in France, followed by an examination of how power is currently distributed within the financial heart.

Strategic investors and alliance-building

The recent history of the French economy highlights the considerable impact of transfers of corporate ownership between the public and private sectors. These transfers reshape the contours of the financial heart and, in each instance, provide opportunities for the principals involved to enhance their competitive positions.

1.   When the parliamentary majority changed in 1986, it triggered considerable shock waves by setting in motion an ambitious programme of privatisation. The overriding objective was to return the largest banking and financial groups to private hands, and to do so on suitable terms and by appropriate means. Those promoting the privatisation of state-owned companies wanted no part of a reference-shareholder model that could open the door to foreign take-overs, nor did they want a model of control by the financial market, since it was believed that French groups lacked sufficient equity capital to resist the likely take-over bids.

It was then that the stable-core model was advanced for the purpose of protecting corporate managers from raiders' assaults. This system, which turns select shareholders into strategic partners, was soon bolstered by a web of circular shareholdings to provide even more effective protection -- if such were possible -- for incumbent managers. The *closed inner core* then became the norm each time a firm was privatised, even during the second period of "cohabitation".

Inter alia, this system offered the advantage of rendering unassailable the mangers ensconced by the authorities shortly before their firms were put on the market.

During the first period of "cohabitation", the financial heart was reconstructed and diversified. Alongside a (still substantial) publicly-owned complex, there emerged another complex -- that of Société Générale and Alcatel. This alliance, which enjoyed strong political backing, shook up the traditional interaction between the Suez and Paribas groups.

The private sector's expansion within the financial heart was to be put on hold, however, between March 1988 and March 1993, when the returning Socialist government's policy was no nationalisation and no privatisation. Naturally, there were attempts to reshuffle the shareholder base of a number of companies; some (like the one involving Société Générale) failed, while others (*e.g.* Havas) resulted in a new configuration. However, this period afforded an opportunity to tidy up and restructure the public-sector financial complex (*e.g.* reciprocal ties between BNP and UAP, the Caisse des Dépôts et Consignations' investment in Crédit Lyonnais, etc.).

2. The second period of "cohabitation" would relaunch the privatisation process with a vengeance. Once again, the impact on the financial heart was substantial. With the transfer of BNP, UAP and Elf Aquitaine to the private sector, the process enabled the Suez complex to reshape its alliances.

    Two very important events were triggered by the dynamic set in motion in March 1993: power was redistributed at Canal Plus, and thus toward Havas, leading to strategic ties between Compagnie Générale des Eaux, Société Générale and Havas; in addition, there was a change in the backing of Assurances Générales de France (AGF), which reduced its cross-shareholdings with Crédit Lyonnais and increased those with Société Générale.

3. With the virtually total dismantling of the public-sector financial complex, of which only Crédit Lyonnais still remains today, the configuration of the financial heart changed in 1994, giving way to two complexes, each a mirror image of the other. Indeed, each can be seen to possess identically complementary lines of business: finance,

banking, insurance, industry, multi-service groups (water), energy, etc.

In this new environment, the outcome of the 1995 presidential election was seen as a strong signal to relaunch projects, since it suddenly widened strategic horizons, with each complex determined to consolidate its positions by intensifying internal concentration. The attempts by UAP and BNP to forge closer ties with Suez, along with Paribas' take-over of Compagnie de Navigation Mixte, were symptomatic of this trend.

4.   UAP's merger into the Axa group was unquestionably the largest financial operation ever transacted in the French stock market. It has placed the new entity at the centre of the French financial heart by establishing a strong connection between its two major complexes. This dominant, asymmetrical position is thoroughly new; will the rest of the banking and financial community accept it? This last move prompts a closer look at the current configuration of the French financial heart and the outlook for its future[5].

The financial heart and the power structure

The end of 1996 was therefore marked by a merger of exceptional proportions between France's two largest insurance groups -- UAP, which had recently been privatised, and Axa, a mutual insurer. Following Axa's public offer to exchange shares, UAP shareholders received two Axa shares for every five of their shares in UAP.

The merger of the two groups gave rise to the world's largest insurer (in terms of assets under management), with perfect complementarity abroad:

- UAP has a strong presence in Europe, with prominent subsidiaries in the United Kingdom (Sun Life), Germany (Colonia/Nordstern) and Benelux (Royal Belge).

- Axa, in contrast, has sought positions in other continents, with Equitable in the United States and recently National Mutual in Australia, thus opening the doors to Asia via Hong Kong.

Of particular interest in this reconfiguration is the dilution of BNP's interest in the new group (to 5.9 per cent) and the fact that Axa-UAP has maintained a substantial stake (13 per cent) in BNP. The asymmetrical nature of this cross-shareholding may be a destabilising factor for the bank. It should also be noted that, prior to that operation, UAP and its partner BNP had embarked upon a process of diluting their cross-shareholdings by absorbing subsidiaries -- Compagnie d'Investissements de Paris in BNP's case (UAP's interest dipping from 14.37 to 14 per cent), and UAP International, boosting the number of UAP shares by 7 per cent.

Lastly, a few weeks earlier, and as a prelude to the merger, the Italian insurer Generali had split with its partner Axa and sold its 11 per cent interest to the group holding company (Finaxa), Mutuelles Axa and Axa SA itself.

Axa-UAP Merger
15 November 1996

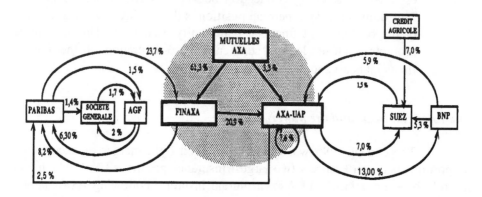

Source: François Morin, SISIFE database (LEREP).

This move substantially restructured the financial heart, in that the new merged entity occupied strategic positions in both major complexes.

- *The Paribas complex*

The first complex is the one that is now headed by five large groups interconnected by a system of circular shareholdings. The closed inner cores include a major bank (Société Générale), France's number-two insurer (AGF), the leading financial corporation (Paribas), an international-scale industrial group (Alcatel Alsthom) and the world's largest multi-service group (Compagnie Générale des Eaux).

78

Through "polarising" shareholdings, the new configuration draws other large groups of the French economy into its strategic orbit, including Total (a major player in the energy sector) and Havas (the leading French multimedia group).

In 1996, the complex was affected by two events in particular. AGF, Consortium de Réalisation (CDR) and GAN together sold off 6.8 million shares in Total (3 per cent of the oil company's total equity) -- a divestment made possible by a change in the June 1992 shareholder agreement. In addition, Saint-Gobain has been gradually acquiring the Poliet group -- France's number-one materials distributor -- from Paribas.

- *The Suez complex*

The second complex has been in existence somewhat longer. It encompasses the same areas of business as the previous complex but is organised differently. At the head of the configuration, also tied together by circular shareholdings there are: a major bank (BNP), the largest group in the energy sector (Elf Aquitaine) and a particularly powerful financial group (Suez), even if the latter is currently experiencing some problems of adjustment.

Other leading French groups can be included in this same orbit by virtue of shareholdings that can also be described as polarising: foremost among them is the minority interest through which Suez now controls Lyonnaise des Eaux-Dumez, France's (and the world's) second-largest multi-service group. This complex is also heavily involved with large companies that are still candidates for privatisation (*e.g.* Air France) or further privatisation (*e.g.* Renault).

In 1996, a number of important transactions altered the organisation of the complex. The French Government sold its 9.1 per cent stake in Elf Aquitaine; half of the shares were bought by French and foreign institutional investors, and the other half was purchased by Elf Aquitaine itself, thereby increasing its treasury stock to 5.2 per cent of issued capital.

Other transactions involved shareholdings in Compagnie de Suez, with Crédit Agricole strengthening ties with Suez by raising its stake to over 6 per cent. Lyonnaise des Eaux and Total dismantled their financial connections, with Total selling Lyonnaise des Eaux its 20.6 per cent stake in

Elyo and Lyonnaise des Eaux selling its 0.8 per cent interest in Total to Cogema.

But at the end of 1996, a vast restructuring of the French industrial sector, tied in with privatisation, was in the works:

- the merger between GEC Alsthom and Framatome, which would give rise to a large equipment-making complex in the civil nuclear engineering sector. Framatome, a former Empain Schneider group subsidiary that has been State-owned since the mid-1980s, has for years been a target of Compagnie Générale d'Électricité, which has since become Alcatel Alsthom.

- the merger between Matra and Thompson (now in doubt), which would forge a international-sized group in the defence industry;

- the merger between Aérospatiale and Dassault Aviation, in military aviation.

These last mergers are extremely complex. Because they are unlikely to take the approach we have examined so far -- that of a closed inner core -- and will probably involve reference shareholders, they raise once again the question of the choice of ownership model for the French financial heart.

Today, while still pivotal in the organisation of strategic alliances, the closed inner core model would seem to have exhausted its potential for restructuring, and its capacity to protect and legitimise corporate management.

Conversely, as part of a plan to divest non-strategic assets, the Elf Aquitaine group sold its interest in Compagnie Générale des Eaux (1.4 per cent as of 31 December 1995). But the group also cut its ties to the Suez group: it sold its 2.9 per cent stake in Compagnie de Suez (to GBL's Electrafina subsidiary), and, in turn, Générale de Belgique (a Suez subsidiary) divested virtually its entire holdings in Elf.

Can French capitalism evolve toward another model of governance -- such as that of a financial market economy in which corporate managers are protected because their firms have sufficiently imposing market capitalisation to ward off raiders and speculators? Or will it go back to a capitalism of reference shareholders in which responsibilities for monitoring management are clearly delineated? The outcome of the major restructuring currently sweeping through the financial heart, as well as the results of forthcoming privatisation, should soon provide a clear answer.

The French financial heart
December 1996

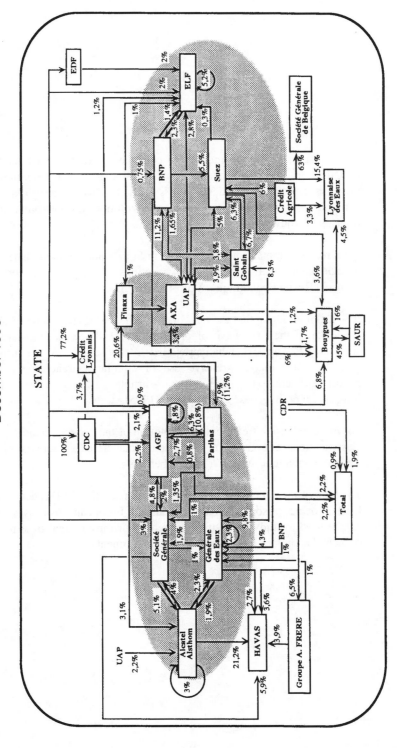

NOTES

1. For a discussion of the models of corporate governance associated with privatisation, see the special issue of La Revue Économique, "Les privatisations : un état des lieux", Vol. 47, November 1996 and, in particular, our article "Privatisation et dévolution des pouvoirs : le modèle français du gouvernement d'entreprise".

2. For a recent summary of privatisation in France and its main characteristics, see Goldstein, A.E. (1996), "Privatisations et corporate governance en France", Revue Économique, Vol. 47, November.

3. It is striking to note that the networks of alliances that were reconstituted in the wake of the first wave of privatisation (1986-88) had structures very similar to the ones that had prevailed in the 1970s. At the time, those structures also made extensive use of circular shareholdings. For the historical context, see our article "Le cœur financier français : morphogenèse et mutation" (1995).

4. For more extensive treatment of the notion of the "coeur financier", see our classifications appearing in "Liaisons financières et acteurs systèmes", Revue Économique, Vol. 47, November 1994.

5. The bulk of the data that follow were taken from the SISIFE database. This LEREP-owned resource covers the largest European business groups and can be used to study their strategic behaviour through real-time monitoring of their shareholder base, contracts and investments.

BIBLIOGRAPHY

ALBERT, M. (1994), "L'irruption du Corporate Governance", *Revue d'Économie Financière*, No. 31.

CHARREAUX, G. (1994), "Conseils d'administration et pouvoirs dans l'entreprise", *Revue d'Économie Financière*, No. 31.

Commission des Opérations de Bourse (COB) (1995), "Marchés 2001", *Les entretiens de la COB*, February.

Committee on the Financial Aspects of Corporate Governance (1992), "Cadbury Report".

DOMPE, M.-N. (1995), "Les pouvoirs dans l'entreprise", Report by the Fourth Round Table, *Les entretiens de la COB*, February.

FAMA, E.F. (1980), "Agency Problems and the Theory of the Firm", *Journal of Political Economy*, Vol. 88.

FAMA, E.F. and M.C. JENSEN (1983), "Separation of Ownership and Control", *Journal of Law and Economics*, No. 26.

FURUBOTH, V.*E.G.* and S. PEJOVITCH (1972), "Property Rights and Economic Theory: A Survey of Recent Literature", *Journal of Economic Literature*, Vol. 10, No. 4, December.

GOLDSTEIN, A.E. (1996), "Privatisations et corporate governance en France", *Revue Économique*, Vol. 47, November.

GROSSMAN, S. and O. HART (1988), "One Share-One Vote and the Market for Corporate Control", *Journal of Financial Economics*, Vol. 20, pp. 175-202.

HARRIS, M. and A. RAVIV (1988), "Corporate Control Contest and Capital Structure", *Journal of Financial Economics*, Vol. 20, January-March, pp. 55-86.

HARRIS, M. and A. RAVIV (1989), "The Design of Securities", *Journal of Financial Economics*, Vol. 24, pp. 255-287.

JENSEN, M.C. and W.H. MECKLING (1976), "Theory of the Firm: Managerial Behavior, Agency Costs and Ownership Structure", *Journal of Financial Economics*, Vol. 3, October, pp. 305-360.

LAFFONT, J.J. and J. TIROLE (1991), "Privatization and Incentives", *Journal of Law, Economics and Organization*, 7(0), Special Issue, pp. 84-105.

LEIBENSTEIN, H. (1966), "Allocative Efficiency Versus X-Efficiency", *American Economic Review*, Vol. 56, No. 3, June, pp. 392-415.

MORIN, F. (1996), "Privatisation et dévolution des pouvoirs : le modèle français du gouvernement d'entreprise", *Revue Économique*, Vol. 47, November.

MORIN, F. (1995), "Le cœur financier français : morphogenèse et mutation", *Marchés et Techniques Financières*, No. 72, July-August.

PASTRÉ, O. (1969), "Le gouvernement d'entreprise : questions de méthode et enjeux théoriques", *Revue d'Économie Financière*, No. 31.

PEJOVITCH, S. (1969), "Liberman's Reform and Property Rights in the Soviet Union", *Journal of Law and Economics*, Vol. 12, April.

PEYRELEVADE, J. (1993), *Pour un capitalisme intelligent*, Grasset.

Revue Économique (1996), "Les Privatisations : un état des lieux", Vol. 47, November.

SAPPINGTON, D.E. and J.E. STIGLITZ (1987), "Privatization and Incentives", *Journal of Policy Analysis and Management*, Vol. 6, No. 4, Spring, pp. 567-582.

SHAPIRO, C. and R.D. WILLIG (1990), "Economic Rationales for the Scope of Privatization" in *The Political Economy of Public Sector Reform and Privatization*, Westview Press, Boulder and London, pp. 55-87.

SIMON, H. (1991), "Organizations and Markets", *Journal of Economic Perspectives*, Vol. 5, No. 2, Spring.

VICKERS, J. and G. YARROW (1991), "Economic Perspectives on Privatization", *Journal of Economic Perspectives*, Vol. 5, No. 2, pp. 111-132.

VOISIN, C. (1992), "Nature et légitimité des entreprises publiques : vers un renouvellement du débat", *Cahiers de recherche de l'équipe dynamique des acteurs et des systèmes en économie ouverte*, No. 7, Spring, Université de Paris Sud.

WILLIAMSON, O. (1991), *The Economic Institutions of Capitalism*, The Free Press, New York.

WILLIAMSON, O.E. (1984), "The Economics of Governance: Framework and Implications", *Zeitschrifts für die gesamte Staatswissenschaft*, No. 140, pp. 195-223.

CORPORATE GOVERNANCE AND PRIVATISATION VIA INITIAL PUBLIC OFFERING (IPO)

by

Tim Jenkinson
Oxford University

Executive summary

1. Governments typically have multiple objectives when privatising firms via a stock market initial public offering (IPO). These include:

    – *maximising revenue*
    – *wide share ownership*
    – *government credibility* (since governments typically conduct a *programme* of privatisation the failure of one sale may impact upon all subsequent sales)
    – *effective corporate control*

    In practice, these objectives often conflict; in particular the political aim of widening share ownership typically conflicts with the economic aims of maximising revenue and encouraging effective corporate control.

2. There are many techniques that can be used to achieve these objectives when privatising. The main choices involve:

    – the *method of sale* (public offer, tender, bookbuilding etc.)
    – whether to use *price stabilisation*
    – whether to allow *part payment*
    – and whether to use *staged sales*.

    The weight given to the various objectives will, to a great extent, determine the techniques chosen to effect the privatisation IPO. The technique chosen then has important implications for the effectiveness of corporate control post-privatisation.

3.   However, effective corporate control depends not only on the way the company is privatised - for example whether the government seeks to encourage small retail investors - but also upon the operation of the market for corporate control in the particular country. In the case of the UK - with its free market for corporate control and high incidence of hostile takeovers - there has been frenzied takeover activity involving privatised companies. For example, of the 12 regional electricity companies privatised in 1990, 10 have now been acquired by other companies (6 of whom are US companies). In countries where there are few structural or technical impediments to takeover, the encouragement of wide share ownership does not necessarily conflict with corporate control being exercised by investors.

4.   For those privatised companies that have market power - in particular utilities - governments will themselves want to retain control over their behaviour post-privatisation. For this reason governments often appoint regulators to exercise this control. However, it is not uncommon for effective regulation to conflict with the unfettered operation of the market for corporate control. Mergers and takeovers can result in a deterioration of information to the regulator as well as pose competition policy concerns. In practice, therefore, regulators may oppose takeovers and exercise control directly (via regulatory intervention or license amendments) or indirectly via the threat of such action. The experience of the UK is that such control by regulators can have far reaching effects upon firms long after they are privatised.

Introduction[1]

Privatisations constitute a particular class of initial public offerings (IPO) where the vendor is not an entrepreneur (or private investor) but rather the government. The main beneficiary of a privatisation is usually the treasury, rather than the company itself, although privatisations are often accompanied by financial restructurings of the companies concerned. In selling previously publicly owned companies governments essentially undertake a debt-equity swap: raising money from the sale of the equity to private investors which reduces the accumulated debt of the public sector. The general public should, as a result, enjoy lower taxes in the future, although collectively they no longer have any claim on the assets sold.

However, the longer term benefits of privatisation are likely to depend upon whether the process of transferring ownership to the private sector provides stronger incentives to efficiency than existed under public ownership. This will itself depend upon the effectiveness of the capital market in exercising corporate control, and, in the case of those companies with natural monopoly elements such as utilities, the efficiency of economic regulation. This paper considers these issues drawing upon international evidence and, in particular, upon the experience of the extensive UK privatisation programme.

Privatisation programmes exist in most countries around the world. One of the most far reaching programmes has been that of the UK where virtually all public enterprises (including most of the utility industries) have now been sold via IPOs. Over the period from 1980-1995 over £61 billion has been raised by the government.

However, whilst the UK may have been an early pioneer of privatisation, its popularity has spread widely in recent years, as can be seen table 1 where the estimated privatisation proceeds for the period 1993-1995 are presented for a number of European countries.

Table 1 **Privatisations in Europe**

	1993	1994	1995
Austria	0.6	1.5	1.9
Belgium	1.1	1.5	0.5
Denmark	0.2	5.7	0.3
Finland	0.2	0.9	0.2
France	8.1	10.7	9.9
Germany	0.5	1.1	4.7
Greece	0.0	0.2	0.0
Italy	2.3	9.0	6.5
Netherlands	0.8	3.9	1.7
Norway	0.2	0.2	0.2
Portugal	0.5	1.1	1.9
Spain	3.0	3.2	2.3
Sweden	0.8	3.4	2.0
UK	8.0	8.5	8.5
Total Europe	**25.8**	**50.8**	**40.5**

Source: Nat West Securities, quoted in Financial Market Trends, OECD, February 1995.

Governments often attempt to achieve multiple objectives via privatisation. These objectives, and how they conflict, heavily influence the way that governments choose to effect privatisation via IPO. The effective corporate control of the privatised enterprises is one possible objective, but there are often other objectives to which governments attach higher political (and possibly economic) priority. This paper starts by outlining the main privatisation objectives, before considering, in section 2, the various techniques available to governments conducting a privatisation programme. In section 3 we consider specific issues relating to corporate control and also the regulation of privatised firms that possess market power, before drawing conclusions in section 4.

1.   Privatisation objectives

There are some important ways in which privatisation IPOs may differ from those conducted by private sector companies. Governments often use privatisations to achieve multiple, often conflicting objectives, some of which are concerned with broad public policy issues. This section explores the impact of these various objectives on the way privatisation IPOs have been structured.

Objective 1: Revenue raising

Revenue raising is the most obvious objective of many privatisations. Governments are able to use privatisation proceeds to reduce public borrowing, which may result in reduced taxation in the future. However, it should be noted that governments also lose a claim on the net cash flow generated by the companies sold, and so taxes will only be lower in the future if the sale proceeds exceed the net present value of the future earnings that would have been earned under public ownership. In practice it will be difficult to know whether this condition is satisfied, although in many cases the net cash raised for the public purse from privatisation (taking account of balance sheet restructurings before the sale) have been quite limited. Clearly, the value of any firm that is sold will reflect investors' expectations of *future* profitability, taking account of any anticipated efficiency savings resulting from the transfer into private ownership. What is noticeable in the case of many privatisations is that, unlike private sector IPOs, the longer term performance of the companies has often been extremely strong, suggesting that at the time of the IPO investors were not aware of the extent of the inefficiencies present under public ownership. This suggests that quite apart from the more technical

90

considerations about how privatisation IPOs should be conducted, government should attempt to rationalise and improve efficiency as much as possible before the sale of the company, in order to appropriate as many of the gains as possible for taxpayers rather than the initial shareholders. A further implication may be that some form of "claw back" of unanticipated profits should be considered, although such provisions will inevitably depress the initial sale price (although this effect will be outweighed in the event of such unanticipated profits[2] materialising). An alternative approach, which we consider more fully below, is the use of staged sales, so that the government retains an equity interest in the future performance of the company.

Discounts on IPOs are essentially transfers between the original owners of the company and those that are allocated shares at the IPO. In the case of a privatised company the initial owner is the government, and the wealth transfer that takes place in the event of the IPO being discounted is between taxpayers in general and the initial shareholders. These wealth transfers will often be *ad hoc*, depending on who participates in the privatisation IPO and who is allocated shares in the event of over-subscription, and will frequently be regressive, with wealthier members of society participating to a greater extent that those with few financial resources to invest in the IPO. As a consequence, one aim of governments should be to maximise the proceeds of the flotation, although governments differ considerably in the vigour with which they pursue this objective.

Objective 2: Wide share ownership

Privatisations have been used by many governments to encourage participation in the stock market by individual investors. It is not entirely clear, however, why this should be a public policy objective. The UK government state explicitly that 'the promotion of wider and deeper share ownership -- both among employees and the general public -- is part of the Government's policy of extending the ownership of wealth more widely in the economy, giving people a direct stake in the success of British industry, and removing the old distinctions between "owners" and "workers".' (H.M. Treasury 1995, p. 4). Some have argued[3] that if wide share ownership is a public policy aim it is more efficiently achieved via the provision of tax breaks to equity ownership, perhaps taking the form of a certain amount of dividend income and capital gain arising from equity investment being tax free each year.

The latter objective of encouraging workers to have a stake in their companies clearly has much more substance, and may contribute significantly to increased efficiency. However, it is worth noting that standard portfolio theory would suggest that individuals, who already have significant amounts of human capital invested in the company they work for, should actually diversify their equity portfolio to include companies other than the one they work for in order to reduce risk. Whilst the encouragement of employee share ownership may have excellent incentive effects, it nonetheless may encourage an inefficient allocation of investment funds.

Many countries include wide share ownership as a key objective of privatisation but few have pursued the objective as vigorously, or for as long, as the UK. Evidence from the UK suggests, however, that after over 15 years of privatisation, share ownership, while wider, is not deeper, and that few additional investors have regularly bought non-privatisation shares. For example, the number of small shareholders in 1979 numbered around 3 million, rising to around 11 million in 1991 before falling back to just over 9 million in 1993. However, according to the partly government-funded Pro-Share, which tracks share ownership, 72 per cent of all retail investors hold shares in only one or two companies. The clear evidence is that many of the early privatisations, which were discounted very heavily, simply induced staging by retail investors. For example, the British Aerospace privatisation in 1981 attracted 26 000 retail investors, although soon after the sale the number of small investors had fallen to just 3 000. More recently, the privatisation of the 12 regional electricity companies in 1991 resulted in 35 per cent of retail investors selling their shares within the first month of trading.

Moreover, from the theoretical perspective the wide share ownership objective can create problems. Many of those potential investors who are the target of government attempts to broaden the shareholder base will often be relatively uninformed, certainly in comparison with institutional investors. The existence of investors with diverse information will inevitably result in winner's curse problems, with the result that discounts will have to increase in order that uninformed investors earn a reasonable rate of return. Hence attempts to broaden share ownership are likely to be directly in conflict with the realisation of revenues that are close to asset valuations.

It is possible that some of these problems can be avoided, or at least reduced, by giving preferential allocations to individual investors in the event of excess demand for the privatisation shares. Many recent privatisations have used multi-part offerings with a book-building exercise aimed at institutional shareholders operating alongside a domestic public offer, for example. Governments often employ a "claw-back" technique whereby if the public offer is over-subscribed then less stock is allocated to institutional investors. This biasing of allocations in the event of excess demand should certainly help to increase the expected returns to the relatively uninformed investors, although it will not remove the negative returns that may occur if an issue is under-subscribed.

Objective 3: Government credibility

Whatever the weight given to the various objectives of government in privatising -- and these vary greatly across countries -- there is a fundamental difference between privatisations and IPOs conducted by private sector companies. Unlike private companies for whom an IPO is a one-off event, governments typically own a whole range of assets that can be sold off sequentially as part of a privatisation *programme*. As a result, individual privatisations cannot be viewed in isolation: a government may, quite rationally, want to invest in a reputation (for instance, for selling companies at fair prices) during the early phases of a privatisation programme, to encourage investor participation in later stages. There have been many examples of government privatisation programmes being set back significantly by an over-priced issue, or by a company that performs poorly in the after-market. For example, the Spanish privatisation programme started running into difficulties in 1995 following the poor performance of previous privatisation offerings (for example, Argentaria's share price had fallen by around 35 per cent since its sale in November 1993). In order to reverse negative investor sentiment it was necessary for the government to re-stimulate interest in the privatisation programme, and it chose, in addition to discounting the shares in the next sale -- Repsol -- to offer investors a one-year money back guarantee, which would compensate investors for any losses up to 10 per cent (we discuss such schemes more fully below). The important lesson is that investors can quickly become disillusioned with privatisations and that the cost to a government, especially one in the early stages of an extensive privatisation programme, of losing credibility may be considerable, and may be difficult to reverse. Consequently, governments rightly place importance on privatisations being viewed as a "success", although, as will be discussed more fully below, there are various ways of promoting the participation of investors that are more sophisticated than simply underpricing the shares by an enormous amount.

The importance of government reputation may also influence the *structure* of privatisations. Even after a firm is privatised it may still by vulnerable to changes in government policy. The most obvious examples of these problems relate to industries that are still regulated by government after privatisation, such as many utility industries (discussed in section 4). In these cases there may be advantages to the use of staged-sales, whereby the government retains a stake in the company for some period of time. The retention of an equity interest should reduce the temptation to change policy in a way that would reduce the value of the firm, and should therefore increase the confidence of potential investors in the credibility of government policy.

Objective 4: Effective control

One of the main arguments for privatisation is that control is shifted from the public sector to private capital markets. Companies are required to report in a standard format to investors on a regular basis and are subject to the analysis and criticism of investors and analysts. However, there are two concerns that arise regarding the effectiveness of the corporate control mechanism for privatised companies.

First, wide share ownership may have detrimental control implications. A large number of very small shareholders may provide little effective monitoring of management, principally due to free-rider and co-ordination problems. However, in practice, institutional investors soon come to dominate the share registers of most privatised companies, so this argument should not be over-stated.

Second, in many cases governments retain a special share in the company that bestows certain control rights. Examples include the "golden shares" existing in many UK privatised companies and the "noyeaux durs" -- or "hard nuts" -- owned by the French government. These special shares are put in place for various reasons -- for example to protect certain industries deemed to be of strategic importance from foreign takeover -- but their effect is inevitably to weaken the corporate control exercised by the capital market. In many cases such shares may remove entirely the threat of a hostile takeover, which in some countries is likely to be far more potent as a threat than the direct intervention of investors. However, some special shares are of limited time duration, and in some cases governments have waived their control rights when a change in corporate control has been proposed (for example in the case of Ford's takeover of Jaguar). It should also be remembered that governments rarely allow the capital market a completely free hand in corporate control, as competition and industrial policy (whether exercised at the national or supranational level) will frequently constrain potential mergers and changes in ownership.

2.   Privatisation techniques

2.1   Methods of sale

Public offers

Most privatisation issues contain a public offer of the shares. The form that public offers take differs considerably across countries, but most are directly aimed at involving small shareholders, with some also embracing larger institutional shareholders. Many early privatisations, such as the early UK offers, were conducted entirely through public offers, with no segmentation of the offer into different components aimed at institutional and/or foreign investors. The advantage of public offers is that they can be used to promote wide share ownership as all members of the public are invited to participate in the offer. However, there are a number of drawbacks with privatisations conducted solely through a public offer.

First, pricing the issue can be extremely difficult. There may be relatively little information available to the government or its advisors as to the likely demand for the shares and hence the appropriate issue price. Some of the most spectacular examples of underpricing have resulted from privatisation public offers, and as a result there has been a tendency towards the use of techniques that allow information about demand to be gathered before the price is set, rather than simply setting the price and waiting to see the extent of demand.

Second, in many countries, the price in a public offer has to be set some considerable time (typically five to ten days) before the shares are allocated, so that investors have time to receive the final prospectus and submit their bids. Such a time delay exposes the issue to much uncertainty, not least regarding movements in the stock market as a whole between the date the price is set and the final date for applications. A particularly graphic example of such problems was the sale of the second tranche of British Petroleum by the UK government in October 1987. The price for the issue was set just before the stock market crash, and the underwriters (in particular the US underwriters who were not able to sub-underwrite the majority of their allocation) were left with sizeable losses as the public refused to subscribe to the offer.

Third, since public offers aim to encourage the participation of retail investors the marketing costs of such issues are often large. Many governments appear, however, to view such marketing as an investment in furthering a public policy goal of promoting wide share ownership.

As a result of these, and other, problems there has been a trend in recent years towards the use of multi-part offerings with a public offer aimed at retail investors and a tender or book-building exercise aimed at larger investors. In such cases it has become normal for the public offer price to be set following the completion of the book-building or tender, which should allow for more accurate pricing. Typically, the public offer price would be set a little below the price established for institutional shareholders -- to encourage wide share ownership -- although other forms of incentives, such as bonus shares or reductions on bills, are frequently offered to retail investors.

Tenders

Some privatisations (for example in France and some UK sales) have been conducted by means of a tender which should, in principle, satisfy the revenue maximisation objective. Pricing privatisations is no easy task, especially given the unique nature of many publicly held firms for whom there are few quoted private sector firms that could be used as comparators to estimate their value. Tenders are a formal way of collecting the markets' collective estimate of the value of the assets, which should be superior to the estimate of any individual investment banker or public servant. However, it is notable that relatively few privatisations are in fact conducted by formal tenders, and, even where they are, the issues are sometimes still priced at a significant discount to the subsequent trading price.

An example of a procedure that was extremely efficient in maximising revenue, and eliciting investors' valuations, was the tender component of the 1987 privatisation of the British Airports Authority (BAA). In common with many recent UK privatisations, the IPO was split into separate parts: an offer for sale (for 75 per cent of the equity) aimed at individual shareholders and a tender offer (for the remaining 25 per cent) aimed at institutional shareholders (although retail investors were not excluded). In the tender offer investors were invited to submit price/quantity bids. The interesting aspect of the tender was that those bids that were successful paid the price *bid*, rather than a common strike *price*. Essentially, the government was able to estimate the entire shape of the demand curve for the issue, and simply picked off the highest bids until all the shares on offer were allocated. In principle, this approach enables the vendor (in this case the government) to appropriate the entire "consumers' surplus". The result was that whilst the fixed price offer was discounted by some 16 per cent, the average price paid under the tender offer was actually slightly higher than the trading price at the end of the first week.

Whilst the BAA example is somewhat unusual in not setting a common strike price, the logic of trying to elicit information from market participants regarding their demand schedules before the issue price is set seems overwhelming. In practice, it is not necessary to sell the entire issue via a tender (which may be unattractive to relatively unsophisticated or uninformed investors); a partial tender, aimed at institutional investors, could be used to determine the issue price, with other techniques used -- such as offers for sale -- to sell the remainder. This approach was adopted by the Japanese Government in the sale of Nippon Telegraph and Telecommunication (NTT), which involved an initial IPO by tender (restricted to institutions) for a relatively small proportion of the equity followed by subsequent secondary issues to which the public could subscribe. The subsequent collapse of the NTT share price (and the large number of individual investors who have incurred losses) should not detract from the attractiveness of such a procedure from the viewpoint of selling public assets at the correct price.

Book-building

A technique that has recently been introduced in a number of markets is book-building. During a book-building exercise investors are invited to submit price/quantity bids for shares with the co-ordinators of the book-building setting an indicative price range for the bids. Book-building is usually targeted at institutional investors. However, in many privatisations the co-ordinators also run a retail book to which individual investors can submit bids, although typically the minimum bid is significantly higher than that defined for the main public offer. There are clearly strong similarities between book-building and traditional tender offers -- indeed the book-building components of recent privatisations in Europe have often been referred to as "International Tender Offers" -- although the way in which the two techniques work differ in significant ways.

First, the type of bid that can typically be made in a book-building is very flexible. A bid could be for a fixed number of shares at a fixed price (as in a traditional tender), or the bid price could be expressed relative to a market index, or could simply be for a fixed quantity of shares at whatever the eventual strike price is. Investors are also required to distinguish between firm bids and indicative bids. Having received all this information, the co-ordinators are then able to establish the likely shape of the entire demand curve and, it is argued, price the issue accurately.

Second, the technique also allows considerable control over who is allocated shares. In the case of privatisations governments will often give preferential treatment to investors who submit "quality" bids. In practice, quality has a number of dimensions including *i)* bids that are firm rather than indicative; *ii)* bids that are submitted early in the offer period (without such discrimination investors would have an incentive to delay submitting their bids until the last minute to keep their options open, and hence little information would be forthcoming for the majority of the offer period); *iii)* bids that are at a specific price (and so contribute to knowledge about the shape of the demand curve, unlike strike price bids); and *iv)* bids that are from investors who are likely to be buyers in the after-market rather than sellers (in order to discriminate in favour of long-term investors rather than those hoping to stag the issue immediately, which might contribute to short-run price instability). The co-ordinators of the IPO are able to discriminate on this latter basis because banks (or other intermediaries) who participate in the IPO are required to disclose the identity of their clients.

Third, in practice a book-building exercise is often accompanied by a much more extensive marketing campaign than traditional issues. This is, in part, because the returns from such efforts are potentially much greater. In a fixed price offering, once it is fully subscribed the only result of effective marketing is to contribute to over-subscription, which in the case of many privatisations has been extreme. However, in the case of book-building, where the price is not set until the last minute, successful marketing can result in a higher price being attained for the IPO, as increased demand will typically result in a higher price rather than greater rationing.

The marketing syndicate is often given strong incentives to market the issue effectively, although this may require careful structuring of commission arrangements. For example, in the US it is commonplace for investors to book their sales through the global co-ordinator even if another member of the syndicate actually performed all the marketing to that particular investor. This is because there is often a belief that the chances of being allocated shares are higher if such a strategy is adopted. One way around this problem is to allow investors to designate to whom commission should be paid, which may or may not be the same syndicate member as receives the order. For example in the case of recent UK privatisations, 20 per cent of the commission has been designated as management commission payable to the syndicate to reflect fixed costs, whilst 80 per cent is related to business brought in. Investors designate which brokers should receive commission and only successful allocations generate commission, so there is no advantage gained by bringing in lots of low quality bids. The result has been strong incentives to perform the marketing, even if the sales are ultimately booked through the global co-ordinator. In the final stage of the British Telecommunications privatisation in 1993, for example, S.G. Warburg -- the global co-ordinator of the issue -- generated 57 per cent of the allocations but only received 36 per cent of the selling commission.

Fourth, a key distinction between book-building and other forms of IPO is that underwriting commissions are avoided, as no fixed price is set until just before the shares are allocated. However, in place of underwriting commissions there will be selling commissions to the syndicate in payment for the marketing of the issue. In the case of recent UK privatisations the selling commissions have been reduced to just one per cent, which compares favourably with those achieved elsewhere.

The main advantage of book-building, therefore, is that the issue is priced *after* a large quantity of information about demand for the shares has been gathered. In principle this should allow the government to set the share price to approximately equate supply and demand. A subsidiary benefit is the control the process allows the government over the allocation of the available shares, with serious long-term investors being favoured over short-term speculative investors. Little of this information would be available in a traditional fixed price offering.

However, despite the many positive aspects of book-building, in practice the results achieved are not always what one might expect from a technique that has a close similarity to a tender. Having gone through the extensive marketing and information gathering stages, governments frequently choose an issue price that generates considerable initial returns. Thus, the politics of privatisation often conflict with one of the main potential benefits of book-building, namely pricing IPOs more accurately.

2.2 Price stabilisation

One of the interesting innovations that has recently been used in a number of privatisations in many countries is price stabilisation. The form that this stabilisation takes varies widely, ranging from intervention in the secondary market by the sponsor in the days or weeks immediately following the IPO to outright price guarantees by the government. In all cases, the main motivation is usually to attempt to reduce short-term share price volatility and in particular to reduce downside risk for investors. We consider in this section the various forms such stabilisation can take.

Over-allotment options

The granting of a call option to the sponsor of an issue, whereby the sponsor is allowed to buy additional shares from the vendor (the government in the case of privatisations) at the issue price, is commonly known as an over-allotment option (or *Green Shoe*, after the US company that first granted such an option). Such options have been used extensively in the US for many years, although only recently have they been utilised in Europe and elsewhere.

The purpose of the over-allotment option is as follows. If there is healthy demand for the shares at the time of the IPO, the sponsor can sell more shares than were allotted in the original offer, thus creating a short position. If prices in the after-market stay above the issue price then no action is taken by the sponsor and the short position is covered by exercising the over-allotment option. Typically, the size of such options is 10-15 per cent of the issue size, although any sized option could be granted. However, the real purpose of the option is to reduce downward pressure on prices in the after-market. If the market price falls below the issue price the sponsor will buy shares to partially, or fully, cover the short position. Since the sponsor only purchases shares at or below the offer price, covering the short position in this way is actually profitable. The ability of the sponsor to stabilise prices is limited by the size of the over-allotment option and the length of time over which the option is granted. A typical over-allotment may last for 30 days, although if the sponsor is confident that the share price will not fall the option may be exercised within this period.

Recent privatisations that have used over-allotment options include the second and third tranches of British Telecommunications (BT2 and BT3), and the second tranche of the UK electricity generators PowerGen and National Power (GenCo2). In the case of BT2 the over-allotment option was partially exercised, implying some price stabilisation occurred, whereas in the case of BT3 the option was exercised in full within the 30 day period covered by the option.

Price guarantees

Over-allotment options can certainly help in limiting short-run downward movements in share prices, and the provision of such (relatively limited) insurance should be valuable to risk averse investors. However, in some recent privatisations price stabilisation has been extended to such lengths that some governments have actually started offering money-back guarantees within a given period. One recent example is Repsol, the Spanish oil group, which announced that if its share price were to fall below the issue price in the year following the sale, it would compensate investors in cash for losses up to 10 per cent. Any fall in excess of 10 per cent would be borne by the investors.

Whilst on first sight this approach seems a rather extreme form of insurance, from the perspective of the issuer it is similar to offering investors a one-for-ten bonus share issue, except that the bonus is not paid at all if the shares remain above the issue price, and will only be partially paid in the event of a fall of less than 10 per cent. Such bonus issues have been used extensively in privatisations in various countries, although in most cases the only contingency has been that the original investor has to retain ownership of the shares for some length of time, rather than being related to share price performance. The obvious advantage of the price guarantee variant of the scheme is that it will be a much cheaper way of providing insurance to risk averse retail investors than a simple bonus share scheme, as well as being more obviously risk reducing to unsophisticated investors.

Hedging via the use of derivatives

The desire of governments to promote wide share ownership combined with the risk averse attitudes of many investors (especially following previous privatisations whose performance has been disappointing) has inevitably resulted in some intermediaries attempting to design schemes that hedge the downside risk. This is especially important in the case of employees of a privatising company, as investing financial capital in addition to human capital in the same company can result in a very undiversified portfolio of assets. A downturn in the fortunes of the company could hence result in an increased chance of workers losing their jobs as well as a reduction in the value of their investments in the company. Since governments frequently seek to encourage employees to participate in a privatisation, the attractions of offering a hedge -- perhaps paid for in part by a less significant discount -- can be considerable.

An example of the type of scheme that has been offered is that devised by Bankers Trust for the French government, who had been frustrated in their aim of encouraging more extensive employee participation in early privatisations. The scheme involved the government using part of the discount it would have offered to members of the employee share ownership plan (ESOP) to buy a hedge against price falls, with the risk being taken on by Bankers Trust. The floor that was placed under the share price meant, in turn,

101

that the shares could be used as collateral against a loan, which could be used to buy additional shares. For each share bought with their own money, investors could buy an additional nine with money borrowed from a bank, with Bankers Trust guaranteeing that the value of the shares would be sufficient to repay the loan. The cost to the members of the ESOP was that they only received any share price appreciation on six out of the ten shares, with the remainder going to Bankers Trust. However, the leveraged nature of the investment meant that potential returns were very high with no downside risk at all.

2.3 *Part-payment*

A technique that has frequently been used in privatisations is that of selling shares on a partly-paid basis. By allowing investors to pay only a proportion of the purchase price at the time of issue the government essentially provides investors with free leverage to their holding. Put another way, the government provides investors with an interest-free loan for the period between the first instalment and the final instalment. Although the shares are traded on a partly-paid basis, their volatility is far in excess of a fully-paid equivalent, as is consistent with standard asset pricing models. For example, compare the behaviour of a fully-paid share valued at 100p and a partly-paid share in the same company with only half currently paid. Good results that increase the fully-paid share price by five per cent to 105p will add the same absolute increase to the partly-paid share price, which should rise from 50p to 55p, producing a 10 per cent return on the investment.

The advantage of employing such schemes from a government's perspective is that even relatively modest premia on privatisation IPOs can become very impressive first day returns when the shares are issued on a partly-paid basis. Part paid investors are also typically eligible to receive the full dividend, which can increase the yield on the partly-paid shares dramatically. For investors wary of the stock market, governments often use such techniques to produce impressive initial returns, although more sophisticated investors should realise that they will subsequently have to pay the remaining instalments upon which there will be zero initial premium. Nonetheless, the implicit interest free loan is certainly an added inducement to invest, and the cost of providing such financing should essentially be viewed as additional implicit underpricing of the IPO.

However there are possible disadvantages from using part-payment schemes. Most significant is that it can encourage staging, with investors able to reap impressive initial returns on the leveraged investment. Certainly, if the intention is to encourage retail investors to participate in the stock market in a long-term and responsible manner (rather than viewing new issues as a source of guaranteed profits) then part-payment schemes appear much less appropriate than long-term incentives schemes. There are many variants of the latter including bonus share schemes for retail investors who hold onto their initial holding for a set period of time, or discount schemes whereby investors receive discounts off their bills (often used in the case of utility privatisations). In some recent privatisations governments have adopted a belt-and-braces approach offering both part-payment and long-term incentives to retail investors. It remains to be seen if such schemes represent money well spent by government, who, as argued above, might be better advised to use such resources to encourage equity investment more generally, for example through the provision of tax-exemptions on a certain amount of dividend income and capital gain accruing on equity investments.

Finally, it should be noted that in some recent privatisations, governments have been prepared to price the subsequent instalments of the shares to reflect the benefits (in terms of leverage and yield) that investors receive from a part-payment scheme. For example, in the sale of the second tranche of the UK electricity generators in 1995 the government issued the shares on a partly-paid basis but set the subsequent instalments such that the fully-paid price was around 6 per cent *above* the trading price of the existing fully-paid equivalent shares. Individual investors were given a discount on the initial instalment in addition to bonus shares or additional discounts for those investors who had registered at "Share Shops" by a particular date. As the UK privatisation programme has progressed there has been an increasing use of incentives tied to establishing broker/investor relationships, which it is hoped will encourage investors to participate in equity investment more generally, rather than concentrating their attention on privatisations.

2.4   Staged sales

Given the problems that many governments have experienced in setting the correct price for privatisations, one obvious response is to conduct the sale in stages. A market price can be established on an initial tranche and subsequent tranches can be sold at more accurate prices later. Numerous governments have adopted the stage sale technique, although it is not always clear that revenue maximisation is the prime justification. We consider below some other objectives that might be achieved by the use of staged sales, but consider first an important problem that can be encountered in using such a technique for privatisations.

Short sales

When privatisations are conducted in stages, with the government attempting to encourage wide share ownership at each stage, a logical problem arises. Given that each tranche will be sold at a discount, with second and further tranches being sold at a discount to the market price, investors should sell their initial holding just before a further tranche is issued, as they can sell at the market price and then buy back at a discount to the market price. But this logic suggests that investors should, where possible, go further and short the issue (sell more shares than they own) and cover the short position by purchases in the next stage of the sale.

However, such behaviour by investors will tend to drive down the market price, which will reduce the revenue accruing to government from the sale of the remaining shares (which are offered at a discount to the market price). Indeed, this problem may be particularly acute during a book-building exercise, as it is in the interest of investors to drive the issue price down towards the bottom of the indicative range only for the price to jump back up following the sale. There have been numerous examples of such problems in both private sector secondary offerings and staged sale privatisations, including allegations of short-selling in the run up to the Eurotunnel and Wellcome secondary offerings in the UK.

There was also much concern at the time of the sale of the third tranche of British Telecommunications by the UK government in 1993 which illustrates graphically the potential problems posed by shorting. S.G. Warburg, the global co-ordinator of the book-building exercise, went to elaborate lengths to ensure that investors who shorted the shares before the offer were denied the opportunity to cover their positions by being allocated shares. Obviously, it is either necessary to have detailed information about share transactions around the time of the offering or to structure the rules regarding trading such that short sales are made less profitable. Both routes were attempted by the co-ordinators, which caused considerable friction with institutional investors. A report by the UK National Audit Office on the sale contains the remarkable fact that the Treasury asked financial regulators to give it information on the identity of those selling BT shares just before the issue, so that they could be denied allocations. However, lawyers advised that this would clearly be illegal and so other less direct methods were employed. The Stock Exchange undertook to monitor large transactions in BT shares just before the issue, and international investors were not told until the last minute how many shares they could buy (this being conditional upon domestic demand), thus making shorting more difficult. Warburg also asked the Stock Exchange to impose immediate cash settlement on BT shares in an attempt to reduce short sales, although the Stock Exchange decided against such a move.

In the event the problems posed by short sales in this case seem not to have materialised, with the BT share price holding its value relative to the market between the date the sale was announced and the ultimate sale. However, governments considering staged sales should take such potential problems seriously. Various options, in addition to those employed above, exist to reduce such problems. For example, regulators could require the immediate publication of short sales in the period before a secondary sale, which would provide the co-ordinators with the required information to discriminate against those with short positions. Less extreme would be publication of the aggregate short position existing in the market as a whole, which could help the co-ordinators judge how much the current market price was being artificially depressed by such actions and price the secondary offering accordingly. A final option might be to regulate short sales in some way, such as the US "up-tick" rule whereby short sales are only allowed when the last movement in the price was upwards. The problem, in any case, is likely to be less pronounced in markets where settlement occurs rapidly.

Wide share ownership

One important reason why governments are often attracted to staged sales is that wide share ownership can thereby be encouraged. Clearly, if individual investors are given significant incentives to apply for shares at each stage, this should increase their participation in the market. This will be particularly effective if the privatised company has performed strongly since privatisation.

However, there is a more subtle reason for adopting staged sales if wide share ownership is a major policy goal. There is some evidence that the attrition rate of small shareholders is lower when the company is sold in stages. An interesting example is the case of British Telecommunications, which was sold in three stages in 1984, 1991 and 1993. After the IPO in 1984 the company had 2.1 million small shareholders, although this number fell to around one million within four years. The second stage of the privatisation resulted in the number of small shareholders rising to 2.6 million, which fell to around 2.2 million before the sale of the final tranche. The 1993 offer increased the number of shareholders to 3.8 million, which by March 1994 had fallen to 2.7 million. Although these figures need to be interpreted with caution, as shareholder eligibility to incentives will have been an important determinant of the timing of sales, there is little doubt that by conducting the sale in stages the government has furthered the cause of wide share ownership. It may also be that the investors in the second and third stages of the sale will be longer term in nature as staging profits are usually rather limited on secondary offerings.

Credibility

A final reason why staged sales may be employed for privatisations is to increase confidence in the minds of investors that the government will not change policy or intervene in ways that would harm the company and reduce shareholders returns. Although in principle privatisation should mean the company being freed from government control, in practice many companies are still highly vulnerable to government policies. The most obvious example of such issues would be in the case of privatised utility industries, where governments typically establish regulatory agencies to control -- at least -- the natural monopoly activities of the privatised company. Although such regulators frequently have the appearance of being autonomous, governments are often able to influence decisions that directly impact on the profitability of the company in numerous ways. By retaining an equity stake in the company, which will subsequently be sold, the government has a direct interest in maintaining the value of the company, at least for some time.

Although it is difficult to distinguish credibility and commitment as the main reason for staged sales, it is remarkable how many privatisations have been conducted on this basis. For example, Chile set out a detailed plan of when the various stages of its privatisation plan would be executed for each company, which typically involved sale of a minority stake followed by further sale(s) at regular intervals. Other countries prefer to sell a controlling stake at the IPO -- to remove the worry that governments will still control the enterprise -- followed by smaller staged sales.

2.5   *Privatisation objectives and techniques*

The previous two sections have discussed the main objectives of privatisation, and the techniques that have been employed by many governments in achieving these various objectives. In this section we attempt to summarise how the various techniques and objectives relate to each other.

Table 2. **Privatisation objectives and techniques**

	Objective			
Technique	*Revenue maximisation*	*Wide share ownership*	*Credibility*	*Control*
Method of sale				
- public offers	✗			✗
- tenders		✗		?
- bookbuilding		✗		
Price stabilisation				
- over-allotments	?			
- price guarantees	?			
Part payment	✗	?		
Staged sales				?

In Table 2 we show, in broad terms, how the four main objectives of privatisation are related to the various techniques available. The classification is inevitably both subjective and refers to broad experience across a number of countries rather than particular privatisations.

Revenue maximisation

In terms of the revenue maximisation objective, there is little doubt that methods involving a *tender* element (which includes book-building) have considerably more potential for reducing underpricing discounts and hence minimising *ad hoc* transfers that can result from privatisation programmes. Public offers, in particular when they are the sole method of sale, typically involve high discounts as risk averse governments, in possession of relatively little information regarding market demand, attempt to ensure that the shares go to a premium. However, it should be noted that large discounts are sometimes observed even when tender or book-building are used. In part this may reflect the government's desire to promote wide share ownership, and could hence be viewed as voluntary. However, at times the initial indicative price range in a book-building exercise can be very wide of the mark, with actual demand being much greater than the co-ordinators anticipated. In this sense, book-building does not entirely remove the importance of establishing the correct price -- in this case a price range -- *a priori*.

Price stabilisation techniques have ambiguous effects upon revenue maximisation. The granting of over-allotments options introduces uncertainty into the final sum raised by the government. In the case of healthy demand the size of the issue can be increased, although it is not clear that this is necessarily in the government's interest as presumably in this case the additional shares that they sell are likely to trade in the market at a premium to the offer price. To maximise revenue the government should retain the shares and sell them later at the market price. In the case of price guarantees, these may be a relatively efficient way of encouraging wide share ownership, and enable the government to reduce the discount on the IPO. They may also be a relatively cheaper way of providing longer term incentives to hold the shares (relative to alternative schemes such as bonus shares) as they only cost the government in the event of share price falls.

Part payment is generally bad for revenue as the government essentially provides an interest free loan over the instalment period. However, in some recent secondary offerings the UK government has actually been able to price partly-paid shares at a premium over the fully-paid price, which reduces the cost of providing such a facility although it also raises the question as to why the government should provide loans for equity investment if they are undertaken on a commercial basis.

Staged sales are generally good for revenue in cases where the post-IPO share price performance is strong, as has often been the case. This is because subsequent tranches of the shares can be sold at higher market prices, and this seems a sensible approach for a government to take if there is a high degree of uncertainty regarding the fundamental value of the assets. Even in cases where the post-IPO performance is average, the discounts offered on secondary offerings are typically much smaller than those observed on privatisation IPOs, which again should enhance revenue for the government.

Wide share ownership

The encouragement of wide share ownership will often result in a *public offer* being an important component of privatisations. Tenders and book-building are typically aimed at institutional investors although it would be possible in countries with a developed system of retail brokers (such as the US) for book-building to be compatible with the encouragement of small investors. *Price guarantees* are likely to be an effective way of encouraging retail investors, who are often both relatively risk averse and in possession of relatively undiversified portfolios. *Part payment* may encourage initial

108

participation but given that the opportunities for staging profits are enhanced may actually discourage the development of long-term shareholders. In contrast, *staged sales* may be a much more effective way of achieving wide share ownership, not only because the government has multiple bites at the same apple, but because there is some evidence that attrition rates for investors in secondary and further offerings are somewhat lower. Again, this is likely to be related to the lower discounts on offer which discourage the stag and leave larger allocations available to investors with a longer time horizon.

Credibility

The credibility of a government's privatisation programme is relatively difficult to establish and easy to lose. High IPO discounts on early privatisations are one of the most obvious (but relatively costly) means by which investors can be encouraged to participate in the programme of asset sales. However, credibility may also be enhanced by the use of *staged sales*, which result in the government retaining an equity interest in the company and hence reduce the incentives to *ex post* appropriation of shareholders' investment. *Price guarantees* may also help to establish, or re-establish, investor confidence, and can be seen as a risk-sharing contract between government and investor.

Control

The privatisation process typically results in a change in the effective control of the company. The various *methods of sale* will have an important impact on how effective investor control is. Public offers will often result in a relatively diverse shareholder base which will tend to provide only weak control over management. Tender offers will generally be targeted at larger or institutional investors -- who should provide more effective corporate control -- although in most cases the government will actually have little information regarding the identity or intentions of the investors. In contrast, the book-building approach certainly provides the government with a much more detailed profile of the potential investors, and should enable discrimination towards investors with longer term interests in the company and hence more commitment towards monitoring and controlling management.

Staged sales clearly provide the potential for government to retain a significant control over management (most obviously when the companies are still majority owned by the government). However, in practice many

109

governments would use such powers extremely sparingly, and some agree to a self-denying ordinance not to vote their shares. The relatively widespread use of special shares, which bestow control rights in certain circumstances, are likely to satisfy many governments' desires to retain a residual control over certain key industries but withdraw from day to day management control.

3.   Corporate control and regulation

The previous two sections have discussed the various objectives governments typically attempt to realise through privatisation and the techniques available to them. Many of the choices made regarding the method of sale will have implications for the subsequent control of the companies when they are in the private sector. For example, the encouragement of wider share ownership may result, initially at least, in a relatively dispersed ownership structure with relatively weak monitoring by investors. However, an initial shareholder register can change rapidly as institutional investors attempt to increase their holdings and, of course, if takeovers or mergers occur. Thus, provided there are not restrictions on the ownership of shares, and/or the ability of other companies to launch a takeover, the capital market should still have a significant impact upon corporate control, even if the company has a large number of small investors.

Of course, countries differ considerably in the extent to which they allow the capital market to operate freely, and this is especially true of privatised companies. As can be seen from Table 3, even the UK, where there are fewer restrictions on (hostile) takeovers than any other country[4] a large proportion of the privatised companies have had special shares that confer certain rights on the government to restrict takeover or the building of significant stakes in the companies. Many of these special shares were time-limited and have now expired, however, and it is also generally true that the government has not chosen to exercise their rights when changes in corporate control have been proposed (for example, Ford were allowed to take over Jaguar). However, the UK government did recently use its special share to block a proposed hostile takeover bid for the largest UK electricity generator (National Power) from a US predator. The important point is that capital market pressures on privatised companies are likely to be relatively weak if ownership is dispersed (due to the objective of wide shareownership) *and* the company is protected by the introduction of special shares that limit the ability of other companies, or investors, to take significant stakes or threaten a takeover.

Particular problems may occur with allowing takeovers in the case of companies that are privatised but have significant market power. The leading examples of such companies are utilities, where governments typically choose to regulate the companies after they are privatised. In such cases there may be difficult conflicts between the goals of corporate control and the ability to regulate effectively, especially in the case of horizontal or vertical mergers within the same industry. In the next section we consider this important class of issues.

3.1   Takeovers of regulated firms

The process of privatising allows the government to influence the initial structure of the industry. As can be seen from Table 3 in the early UK privatisations there was a tendency to privatise whole industries as an integrated whole (for example British Telecom and British Gas) rather than attempt to change the structure of the industry with a view to making the subsequent regulation easier. Later UK privatisations took a different approach with care being taken to introduce, where possible, horizontal competition between firms and vertical separation between different sectors of the industry with the objective of enabling new entry into the potentially competitive parts. Examples of these policies include:

 − the water industry - horizontally separated into 10 large water and sewerage companies and about 20 smaller water-only companies;

 − the electricity industry - which was vertically separated into generation, transmission, distribution and supply, with horizontal separation introduced in distribution, supply and generation;

 − the railway industry - with the vertical separation between running the rail infrastructure (RailTrack), train operating companies, and train leasing companies, and horizontal separation introduced into the latter two areas.

Experience has shown that such separation can help the regulators who are charged with controlling the prices and practices of these industries post-privatisation, not least because the fundamental information asymmetry between regulator and regulatee is reduced to varying extents. However, the remarkable feature of these privatised and regulated sectors in the UK has been the enormous amount of takeover activity that has occurred since special shares have expired. In the table below we document the control changes that have been effected and those that have been attempted but blocked.

111

This takeover activity has resulted in 10 of the 12 regional electricity companies (who have a local monopoly over electricity distribution and are also major players in the increasingly competitive electricity supply business) being taken over. The main predators have been US electricity companies and UK water companies. Indeed, this takeover activity has resulted in the formation of "multi-utility" groups. Examples include:

-   Scottish Power - which is an vertically integrated electricity generator, transmission and distribution company in its Scottish franchise area, and now owns an English electricity distribution and supply company and an English water company

-   United Utilities - which was formed when North-West Water took over its local electricity distribution and supply company to form an integrated regional utility, as did

-   Hyder - which was formed when Welsh Water took over South Wales Electricity.

Government policy regarding these takeovers has not always been consistent. For example, ScottishPower (which is, amongst other things, an electricity generator) was allowed to take over an electricity distribution company, but the other two main UK generators (National Power and PowerGen) were blocked by the government in their bids to take over distribution companies. It is interesting to note in these latter cases that the competition authorities (the Monopolies and Mergers Commission) recommended that the bids should be allowed to proceed as they posed few competition policy problems, but the Secretary of State for Trade and Industry blocked the bids and also prevented a US predator from bidding for National Power. Few convincing reasons were forthcoming for either decision.

In the water sector, there has been a relatively laissez faire approach taken to cross-sector mergers (witness the formation of the multi-utility groups) but the competition authorities have imposed increasingly stringent conditions (including large price reductions) before allowing horizontal mergers to proceed. In an early case, Lyonnaise des Eaux (via their wholly owned North-East Water) were allowed to take over the local water and sewerage company Northumbrian Water, conditional upon significant price reductions. However, in a recent contested takeover battle for South-West Water, involving two rival water companies, the bids were effectively blocked on the grounds that further takeovers would impair the regulator's ability to make yardstick comparisons between firms in the sector.

Table 3
The UK Privatisation Programme

Company	Date of IPO	Proceeds¹ (£ million)	Technique	Proportion retained at IPO (%)	Staged sales 2nd tranche	Staged sales 3rd tranche	Special shares⁴
British Petroleum	11/79	284	OFS	51.0	9/81 T	10/87 OFS & T	yes
British Aerospace	2/81	43	OFS	48.4	5/85 OFS		yes
Cable and Wireless	10/81	181		50.6	12/83 T	12/85 OFS	
Amersham International	2/82	64	OFS	nil			
Britoil	10/82	334	T	49.0	8/95 OFS		
Assoc. British Ports	2/83	46	OFS	48.5	4/84 T		
Enterprise Oil	6/84	384	T	nil			
Jaguar²	7/84	297	OFS	nil			
British Telecom	11/84	3,685	OFS	49.8	12/91 OFS & BB; OAO	7/93 OFS & BB; OAO	yes
British Gas	12/86	3,691	OFS	3.3	7/90 BD		yes
British Airways	2/87	858	OFS	2.5			yes
Rolls Royce	5/87	1,032	OFS	0.4			yes
British Airports Authority	7/87	1,223	OFS & T	4.4			
British Steel	12/88	2,425	OFS	0.1			
10 Water Companies	12/89	3,395	OFS	1.6			
12 Regional Electricity Companies	12/90	3,395	OFS & T³	1.5			
National Power	3/91	1,341	OFS & T³	40.0	3/95 OFS & BB; OAO		yes
PowerGen	3/91	822	OFS & T³	40.0	3/95 OFS & BB; OAO		yes
Scottish Hydro-Electric	6/91	920	OFS & T³	3.5			yes
Scottish Power	6/91	1,955	OFS & T³	3.5			yes
N. Ireland Electricity	6/93	684	OFS	3.3			yes

Source: HM Treasury (1995)

Abbreviations: OFS: offer for sale at a fixed price; T: tender; BB: bookbuilding; BD: bought deal; OAO: over-allotment option granted.

Notes:

1. The proceeds figures include the value of the sale of ordinary shares at the IPO but does not include the value of any debt or preference shares created in the company that are repayable to the government, proceeds from the second and third tranches of staged sales.

2. In the case of Jaguar the proceeds of the sale were retained by its parent company (British Leyland)

3. In these cases the tenders were "back-end" tenders

4. Only special shares that are still in place are noted here. Some special shares were created that expired at certain dates (such as the water companies and the regional electricity companies); others (such as case of Jaguar) were redeemed at the time of a takeover.

Table 4. **Bids for UK privatised utilities**

Company/Sector	New owner	Failed bidder(s)	Reason bid failed
Electricity Distribution			
Eastern Electricity	Hanson		
E. Midlands Electricity	Dominion Resources (US)		
London Electricity	Entergy (US)		
Manweb	Scottish Power		
Midlands Electricity	Avon Energy (US)	PowerGen	market power
Northern Electric	CE Electric (US)		
Norweb	North-West Water		
SEEBOARD	CSW Corporation (US)		
Southern Electric		National Power	market power
South Wales Electricity	Welsh Water		
South West Electricity	Southern Electric Int. (US)		
Electricity Generation			
National Power		Southern Company (US)	unclear
Water			
Northumbrian Water	Lyonnaise des Eaux		
Southern Water	Scottish Power		
South-West Water		Severn Trent Water	undermines yardstick
		Wessex Water	competition

The UK experience, therefore, has been that privatised firms have been the subject of quite frenzied merger and takeover activity since the expiry of their special shares. Of course, this is in no small part due to the fact that the UK capital market, in contrast with most other European stock markets, has a very active market for corporate control working through hostile takeovers. The initial wide share ownership has been no impediment to this process whatsoever. The main issue has been, and continues to be, whether such corporate control changes adversely affect the ability of the regulators effectively to regulate the firms, especially when the regulated firms become part of multi-utility groups, conglomerates or foreign firms. This has led in turn to important license amendments being imposed on such companies and even a call for the separate listing of such companies.[5]

In the next section we consider briefly the role of licenses in controlling regulated privatised companies.

3.2   The use of licenses to control privatised firms

Whilst the capital market may provide a considerable degree of overall corporate control, there remain concerns regarding the ability of government to control particular activities of privatised firms. This is clearly most relevant in the case of those companies that do not face effective competition in some areas of their business, such as utility companies. Issues might include security of supply, transfer pricing, non-discrimination, anti-competitive practices and even, perhaps, dividend policy. Some of the issues can be dealt with via existing competition laws, but in practice many governments have chosen to control privatised firms with market power through the issuing of licenses that define the powers of the regulator and certain rules that the firm has to abide by. Such licenses can be periodically changed by the regulator (subject to consultation and appeal) or by the government.

In practice, such licenses confer considerable powers of control over the activities of the firm even after privatisation. For example, recent license amendments in the water industry (which have accompanied takeovers) have imposed requirements to subject major elements of expenditure to competitive tendering (to guard against companies transferring the profits out of the regulated company through distorted transfer pricing rules), and have required that companies should seek the approval of the Director General of Water Services in respect of their dividend policy.

The threat of license changes can also be extremely effective when regulators want to control the activities of a firm in a particular way. For example, the UK electricity regulator was able to "impose" a price cap on the prices charged by the main electricity generators despite the fact that no such price cap was ever envisaged for electricity generation (although price caps do exist for transmission and distribution). This was "agreed" when the regulator threatened the two main generators who have considerable influence over the electricity spot price in the UK with being referred to the Monopolies and Mergers Commission on the grounds that there was a lack of effective competition in the generation market. As part of the same negotiations the regulator required the generators to dispose of some of their plant to other parties, which has since been completed.

What these episodes show is that the threat of license amendments and/or reference to competition authorities can often been a powerful way of controlling companies even after they are privatised. The regular (5 yearly) reviews of the prices charged by regulated firms (which also result in license amendments) also allow considerable control over the activities and prices charged by regulated privatised firms. The fundamental constraint facing UK regulators is not so much a lack of powers to control or influence privatised firms, but a lack of information regarding the likely future costs, efficiencies and quality of service. Other corporate control changes, such as mergers and takeovers, may adversely affect the information flowing to regulators, and this is probably the main reason why regulators may object to unfettered takeover activity.

4.   Conclusions

Governments often have multiple objectives when privatising firms, and the attempt to achieve these (often conflicting) objectives influences the way they choose to conduct the initial public offering. This paper has suggested that effective corporate control is one such objective, but that three other main objective typically exist: revenue maximisation, wide share ownership and government credibility (which will influence the success of the entire privatisation programme). The methods available to governments choosing to privatise via IPO are numerous, as section 2 discussed, with the choice of technique being a function of the relative weight attached to the various objectives. The technique chosen then has important implications for the effectiveness of corporate control post-privatisation.

However, the effectiveness of corporate control also depends upon the operation of capital markets, in particular whether takeover threats, or other means of monitoring and controlling managers, exist. Government attempts to protect the company from takeover, via the issuing of special shares or other restrictions, will inevitably weaken such control. However, the evidence from the extensive UK privatisation programme has been that takeover activity quickly developed once special shares expired, and that the relatively dispersed shareholder base - resulting from the political goal of wide share ownership - has been no impediment to such takeovers (often of a hostile nature) succeeding. However, such activity reflects the exceptionally free market for corporate control in the UK. In other countries where takeover restrictions, of either a structural or technical nature, are commonplace the objective of wide share ownership may conflict more significantly with effective corporate control.

Finally, for those companies that possess market power and hence require on-going regulation - such as utility industries - it was argued that effective regulation at times conflicts with regulators' ability to monitor and control the privatised firm. Mergers and takeovers can result in a deterioration of information to the regulator as well as posing competition policy concerns. However, control is in practice not simply exercised by the threats imposes by the capital market but also by the threat of regulatory intervention, for example through license amendments or periodic review of prices and rates of return. The experience from the UK privatisation programme is that such control is critical in achieving the various aims of public policy.

NOTES

1. This paper draw upon Jenkinson and Ljungqvist, *Going Public* (Oxford University Press, 1996).

2. An example of such provisions is the claw-back of profits from future property development that may be carried out by Railtrack, the UK railway track operator. Railtrack has been privatised with a large portfolio of land of unknown commercial value. The government has therefore made an assumption as to how much Railtrack will make out of the exploitation of these assets, and any amount up to the assumed sum will be retained by shareholders. Any excess will be shared between shareholders and customers (via reductions in track access charges).

3. See, for example, Jenkinson and Mayer (1988) "The Privatisation Process in France and the U.K.", *European Economic Review*, 34, 482-490.

4. See Jenkinson and Mayer (1994), *Hostile Takeovers*, McGraw-Hill.

5. Most vocal amongst the UK regulators has been Ian Byatt, Director General of Water Services. See also Jenkinson and Mayer (1997), "Regulation, Diversification and the Separate Listing of Utilities", forthcoming in volume edited by Michael Beesley.

THE COSTS AND BENEFITS OF PUBLIC SECTOR HOLDING COMPANIES (PSHC's)*

by
Harry Baumann, Ph.D.
Partner, SECOR

My presentation concerns the costs and benefits of public sector holding companies (PSHC's). As a Canadian, I feel some trepidation about tackling this subject because we have simply made only a modest use of this instrument. In fact, in relative terms, Canada has historically made a modest use of SOE'S as instruments of government policy. Thus, when privatisation came into vogue in the 1980's, I recall having to explain to my political masters that a Canadian privatisation program could never be as "successful" as the one in the U.K. because we simply did not have as many assets to sell. Indeed, at the federal level, the total number of employees of SOE's was just short of 200 000 in the early 1980's and today after the privatisation program, the number stands at 80 000. This compares with a total Canadian labour force of 13 million.

A country with a relatively small SOE sector will also tend to have PSHC's which are few in number and of limited importance for the economy as a whole. Nevertheless, there are some aspects of the costs and benefits of PSHC's based on the Canadian experience which the Conference participants should find of interest.

---

*   I would like to thank my former colleagues at the Crown Corporations Directorate of Treasury Board and Finance Canada, and my current colleagues at the Vietnam-Canada Financial Management Project for their contributions to this document. The responsibility for the content of this document rests with me and not SECOR or the VCFMP

A perspective on public sector holding companies

I should explain that I come to the subject of PSHC's very much as a practitioner. Thus, during the 1980's, I served as Director of Policy for Crown Corporations (which is what SOE's are called in Canada) and as Project Coordinator in the Privatisation Secretariat. In an earlier period, I was involved in the monitoring and funding of SOE's in the energy sector. From this perspective, I found some of the literature which I reviewed for this conference rather unsatisfying. It seemed to me that the commentary on PSHC's was often quite vague and general, and very much process as contrasted with transactions oriented. Moreover, in all the discussion of accountability and control, the researchers in public administration appear to have lost sight of the fact that the SOE's in a PSHC portfolio are expected to deliver goods and services as well as having a public policy role. If the legal and institutional framework does not permit PSHC's to behave in an entrepreneurial way in meeting both commercial and public policy goals, then the observation that the costs exceed the benefits becomes a mere truism.

In organisational terms, the role of the PSHC's in this presentation is circumscribed by a parliamentary system of government where the holding company ultimately reports to a cabinet or a cabinet committee of ministers or possibly to one responsible minister who accounts for its operations to the legislature. (See Figure 1.) Within this context, a lot of variations are possible, but these shall be largely left to the textbooks for further elaboration.

Figure 1. **Organisational overview**

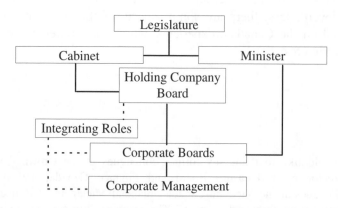

Source: Stevens, Douglas, "Corporate Autonomy and Institutional Control"

The holding company universe

A holding company, whether in the public or private sectors, has common characteristics. Thus, it is a company which owns shares in other companies, usually but not always, in subsidiaries. Moreover, a holding company is a nonoperating company which does not carry out activities such as production or marketing, but rather manages the holdings or the portfolio from a financial and strategic perspective. In broad terms, the holding company seeks to ensure the financial health and performance of its assets and allocates capital according to target returns and strategic considerations.

A public sector holding company (PSHC) may be similar in structure to its private sector counterpart, but in addition to financial objectives, it will usually have one or more public policy roles. This point will be explored further below.

The PSHC may be 100% government owned, or it may be a mixed corporation with some private sector ownership. In the case of a mixed corporation, the private shares may be either closely held or widely distributed.

For the purpose of this presentation, a narrow definition of a holding company and specifically a PSHC will be utilised. Thus, the universe will consist of PSHC's which have a significant share ownership in their subsidiaries and monitor and control them on a continuing basis. Internationally, such PSHC's as IRI (Italy), VEBA (Germany), OIAG (Austria) come to mind.

In Canada, at the federal level the most important PSHC's have included:

- Canada Development Corporation or CDC (Mixed)

- Canada Development Investment Corporation (CDIC)

- Cape Breton Development Corporation (DEVCO)

- Canadian National

At the subnational (provincial) level the most prominent PSHC examples have been or are:

- British Columbia Resources Investment Corporation or BCRIC (transition phase to privatisation)

121

- Société Générale de Financement or SGF (first mixed public/private then 100% government owned)

- Crown Investments Corporation (the classic example in Saskatchewan)

The most outstanding feature of this sample of PSHC's is their great diversity in terms of rationale, objectives, reporting relationship, scope of operations and accountability and control mechanisms. In addition, these characteristics often changed over time as did the PSHC performance in achieving financial targets or meeting public policy goals.

At the federal level, a key question during the 1980's concerned the economic and financial performance of PSHC's and their holdings, that is, SOE's, relative to private sector equivalents, and whether the private sector holding companies could offer some lessons on improving this performance either for the PSHC's or the whole portfolio of SOE's.

It is in this context that the holding company project was undertaken by the Crown Corporations Directorate in the 1980's. In other words, an effort was made to identify the best practices of private sector holding companies, and to examine their applicability for PSHC's, and/or to mimic these practices in the management of the SOE's. In the latter case, the Crown Corporations Directorate of the Treasury Board could be equated to a holding company for those SOE's which were not slated for privatisation.

In the Canadian case, and this may not be true elsewhere, there were some private sector holding companies which could serve as possible sources for best practices. Among these, the following were examined:

- Bell Canada Enterprises (Telecom Services and Equipment)

- Power Corporation (Financial Services, Resources, Infrastructure)

- IMASCO (Financial Services, Tobacco, Hospitality, Trade)

- Claridge or Seagram (Drinks and Media)

- BRASCAN (Diverse, including natural resources, drinks, etc.)

- NOVA (Oil and Gas, Petrochemicals, Pipelines and Services)

Unfortunately, it is impossible to go into detail on the findings of the holding company project. However, it will come as no surprise to anyone that the existence of public policy objectives makes a complete transfer of private sector practices problematic. Moreover, one is almost immediately confronted by the difficulty of providing the same incentives for superior financial performance to the executives of PSHC's as is the practice in the private sector. Nevertheless, such ideas as the issuance of phantom shares to senior management of the PSHC's were considered without, however, finding a feasible scheme for implementation. At the end of the day, the inability or unwillingness to implement the best practices of private sector holding companies in the public sector casts a shadow over the future use of this instrument.

The intended benefits of public sector holding companies

I have used the qualifying adjective "intended" in this subtitle advisedly. Thus, based on experience the sought after benefits have often not been achieved although admittedly a definitive assessment of PSHC's remains part of "unfinished business."

In Canada, with an economy that is biased toward resource industries and which has a large degree of foreign ownership, it was inevitable that various instruments of industrial policy including SOE's would be considered to address these "problems". In turn, the reliance on foreign capital and the absence of "high tech" industries was often attributed to a lack of domestic risk capital.

Given this context, it is perhaps not surprising that someone should hit upon a mixed (public/private) holding company as a solution. Thus, the holding company could start life as 100% government owned and be based on a bundle of state assets with reasonable earning potential. Subsequently, some of the shares in the PSHC could be sold to private investors, especially small individual investors. In addition, over time holding company capital could be reallocated to more risky high tech investments. Ownership of shares in the PSHC was perceived as less risky for the individual investor because of the partial government ownership and because of the diversification of holdings.

The above holding company structure is the theory behind the Canada Development Corporation. In practice, the CDC never lived up to its potential and, far from representing the best of both the public and private sector, it ultimately represented the worst of both. For a number of legal and institutional reasons, the government was never able to exert any influence on the capital allocation decisions of the CDC, yet attempts to do so convinced the investment community that goals other than profit maximisation were being pursued, and therefore that the shares of CDC should sell at a discount.

PSHC's have almost always had industrial or regional development as one of their objectives. The use of a PSHC in shifting capital from resource-based industries to high tech industries has already been noted. More generally, PSHC's may be used to transfer financial and other resources from declining to growth industries. Unfortunately, this strategy implies an ability to pick winners and losers. It is not clear that PSHC's are more capable in this regard than anyone else. Even if one were to redefine the problem to select winning activities rather than winning industries based on some notion of comparative advantage, the problem of selecting the appropriate and ultimately profitable investments remains. One could argue that a PSHC should be more successful on this score than a government department or an operating SOE, but the evidence is far from convincing.

The picture is even murkier in the case of PSHC's dedicated toward regional development. In the case of Canada, a PSHC was used to try and diversify and rejuvenate the industrial base of a declining coal and steel region, namely, Cape Breton. This situation is not unknown in other countries. The advantages of the Canadian case were that the coal and steel region was relatively small, and that the oil crisis of 1974 and 1979 with their impact on coal prices made the whole rehabilitation exercise look somewhat plausible. This is why the evaluations performed on the Cape Breton Development Corporation are often surprisingly positive given its ultimate inability to protect employment in coal mines or steel mills or to diversify the regional economy.

Another intended benefit of the PSHC is to improve the financial management of the holdings (subsidiaries) in its portfolio. This is thought to be especially relevant when the PSHC Board of Directors and its staff or management are dominated by people with private sector experience. In this scenario, it is widely assumed that the SOE's are under the control of responsible ministers who cherish their public policy and not their profit maximisation roles. Thus, the PSHC provides a counterbalance to the desire to achieve public policy objectives through the SOE's. In addition, a PSHC dominated by private sector experience is thought to be an excellent vehicle for introducing private sector techniques in monitoring economic and financial performance within the SOE domain.

In practice, the most significant contribution of PSHC's in financial management has come through their role in managing bailouts and dealing with financial crises. Certainly, in the case of the CDIC, which had numerous roles

124

and objectives ranging from giving advice to governments to facilitating privatisation, the most prominent and memorable role was the bailout and subsequent commercialisation of the aircraft companies (Canadair, de Havilland).

An obvious step after the successful commercialisation of an SOE is the consideration of its privatisation, possibly facilitated through a PSHC. A PSHC with a board of directors that has strong representation from the private sector may be helpful in ensuring that the SOE's in its portfolio are ready for privatisation with an effective management team in place. The PSHC can also play a useful role as advisor for privatisation and identifying acceptable purchasers for the SOE's. In the Canadian case, and this refers largely to the CDIC, problems arose with the PSHC model of privatisation related to concerns from Ministers about the adequate treatment of the public policy roles of the SOE's and possible conflicts of interest among PSHC board members who were also potential purchasers of state assets. The bottom line conclusion of most analysts has been that a PSHC can play a useful role in privatisation, but it must be carefully defined and limited.

The term public/private partnerships has come into vogue recently, but PSHC's have traditionally involved elements of public/private partnership. The most obvious case, as noted above, involves a mixed corporation (CDC), but even in the case of 100% government owned PSHC's there may be joint ventures with private sector partners (*e.g.* SGF). An entirely different element of partnership involves the use of the PSHC board of directors as a source of advice to the government on public policy and program issues. If the board of directors is dominated by private sector members, then there is a tendency for a unidirectional flow of suggestions which can degenerate into a series of complaints about the government's actions or its inaction. However, when the board has effective public sector representation there can also be a genuine back and forth flow of advice; this would appear to be the lesson to be drawn from the case of the CDIC and the CIC. The obvious danger of a public/private partnership is that it ultimately smacks of the corporate state. At a minimum, the business community can obtain through an institution such as the PSHC privileged access to Ministers which is not accorded to the same extent to other groups in society. The issue of the corporate state is usually discussed at the macro level, but it is an obvious concern also at the micro level since the PSHC, as already noted, may be involved in commercialisation and privatisation issues as well as policy advice.

The costs of PSHC's

The direct financial cost of PSHC's is usually very small because, in addition to the board of directors, there is normally only a small of staff consisting of a few key people. In contrast, the indirect cost of a PSHC can be substantial especially if the PSHC and its subsidiaries become involved in bailout and industrial restructuring activities, but the whole idea behind a PSHC is to minimise these costs and to carry out such activities as efficiently as possible. Another indirect cost of PSHCs relates to the fact that they impose another layer of decision-making as illustrated by the organisation chart referred to earlier. (Figure 1.) Thus, someone may argue that the direct costs of a PSHC may be low but the value added is tiny, and hence, the benefit cost ratio is terrible. Needless to say this problem is not unique to the holding companies in the public sector as recent efforts to eliminate or rationalise holding companies in the private sector indicate.

In the Canadian case, corporate restructurings have been carried out with and without the holding company model, and unfortunately no definitive analysis of relative effectiveness exists. The surprising fact is the number of restructurings that have been successful independent of the choice of instrument that has been adopted. As the term bailout suggests, few public policy analysts give much credence to the long term viability of firms caught in a financial crisis requiring restructuring. Nevertheless, it could be worthwhile to analyse successes and failures in corporate restructuring in both the private and public sectors and relate them to the choice of restructuring instrument.

Although PSHC's are often intended to impose private sector financial discipline, they may do exactly the opposite - they may become another curtain to hide behind for the responsible minister, his or her departmental bureaucrats, and of course, the operating SOE's themselves. The extent of the opportunity to avoid accountability depends, of course, upon the precise organisational structure of the PSHC in relation to the other relevant actors.

The final indirect cost falls under the heading "a waste of talent and time". As most officials know, the scarcest resource for cabinet ministers is time. In a parliamentary system, ministers have several roles to play which continually squeeze the agenda. However, PSHC board members are important people and, whether there is an important issue or not, regular meetings will have to be scheduled, which cannot easily be rescheduled. The potential for wasting time is always there even if it has not been a serious problem in practice.

The benefits versus costs of PSHC's

Clearly it is difficult to provide a definitive quantitative assessment of the benefits versus costs of PSHC's. Nevertheless, one can reach some tentative conclusions based on the Canadian experience.

An assessment by company and by objective (or intended benefit) as illustrated in Figure 2 reveals a mixture of positive, neutral and negative results; there are also pluses and minuses within each company and within each objective. Moreover, in the case of long lived PSHC's such as Canadian National there are periods of positive and negative performance both on financial and public policy criteria. Nevertheless, if one had to come to a bottom line on PSHC's based on the Canadian experience, given that there are some measurable direct costs, the balance is slightly negative. A more positive assessment might focus on overall policy results rather than specific transaction costs.

Figure 2. Assessment of benefits versus costs of PSHC's in the Canadian context

An assessment by company	
Canada development corporation	-
Canada development investment corporation	+
Cape breton development corporation	-
Crown investments corporation	0
Canadian national	0
An assessment by objective or intended benefit	
Economic sovereignty	-
Ownership of shares	+
Head office activity	+
Economic development	-
Regional development	=
Financial management	0
Corporate restructuring	+
Privatisation	0
Preparation for privatisation	+
Public/private partnership	0

The future of public sector holding companies

Based on the above analysis, one could hardly recommend the creation of bigger and better PSHC's. Rather, one might suggest the adoption of the best features or practices of PSHC's or their private sector counterparts within SOE's or the relevant units of government ministries, and limit their activities to niche services such as corporate restructuring, financial management and preparation for further commercialisation areas.

SOURCES

Annual Reports of Holding Companies in the Public Sector in Canada: Canada Development Investment Corporation (CDIC), Canada Development Corporation (CDC-Mixed), Canadian National (CN), Cape Breton Development Corporation (CBDC) or Enterprise Cape Breton Corporation.

Annual Reports of Holding Companies in the Private Sector in Canada: Bell Canada Enterprises (BCE), BRASCAN (Edper Investments), Claridge Investments (SEAGRAM), Power Corporation, IMASCO, NOVA.

BAUMANN, Harry, "Lessons of the Canadian Privatisation Experience for Tunisia," Report to the World Bank, August, 1988.

BEESLEY, M. E., A. Liberman and S. Bloomfield, "Controlling Public Enterprises in Europe," Economic Council of Canada, Ottawa, 1986.

BELL, Joel, "Industrial Policy in a Changing World," Towards a Just Society, Tom Axworthy and Pierre Trudeau, eds., Markham, Canada, 1990.

BORCHERDING, THOMAS E. Et. Al., "Comparing the Efficiency of Private and Public Production: The Evidence from Five Countries," Zeitschrift für Nationalökonomie, Supplement 2, 1982 pp. 127-156.

BORINS, S. and B. BOOTHMAN, "Crown Corporations amd Economic Efficiency," Royal Commission on the Economic Union and Development Prospects for Canada, vol. 4, Canadian Industrial Policy in Action, Ottawa, 1985.

BROOKS, Steven, "Who's in Charge? The Mixed Ownership Corporation in Canada," Institute for Research on Public Policy, Halifax, 1987.

BROOKS, Steven, "The State as Entrepreneur: From CDC to CDIC," Canadian Public Administration 26 (Winter 1983) p. 541.

Economic Council of Canada, "Minding the Public's Business," Supply & Services Ottawa,Canada, 1986

FRANKEL, Paul, H., MATTEI: Oil and Power Politics, London, 1966.

GENEEN, Harold, "Managing," Garden City N.Y., 1984.

Government of Canada, "Governor in Council Appointments in Crown Corporations," no date.

GRAVELLE, Hugh S.E., "Incentives, Efficiency and Control in Public Firms," Zeitschrift für Nationalökonomie, Supplement 2, 1982, pp.79-104.

LAUX, Jeanne Kirk and Maureen Appel MOLOT, "State Capitalism: Public Enterprise in Canada," Ithaca and London, 1988.

McFETRIDGE, D.F., "Commercial and Political Efficiency: A Comparison of Government, Mixed and Private Enterprises" Royal Commission on the Economic Union and Development Propects for Canada, Vol. 4, Canadian Industrial Policy in Action, Ottawa, 1985.

NODEN, Janet, "Accountability and Control in the Capital Financing of Federal Crown Corporations." MPA Thesis. University of Victoria, Canada, 1987.

Office of Privatization and Regulatory Affairs, Government of Canada, "Information,", Ottawa, various dates.

OHASHI, T.M. and T.P. ROTH, eds.,"Privatization, Theory and Practice," Vancouver, 1980.

REDWOOD, John and John HATCH, "Controlling Public Industries", London, 1984.

SHEEHAN, Gary, "Presentation to the Delegation from Vietnam on Canadian Crown Corporations and other Corporate Interests," Treasury Board and Department of Finance, Canada, Ottawa, 1996.

STANBURY, W.T. and Thomas KIERANS, "Papers on Privatization", IRPP, Montreal, 1985.

STEVENS, Douglas J., "Corporate Autonomy and Institutional Control: The Crown Corporation as a Problem in Organization Design," Montreal and Kingston, 1993.

Treasury Board, Government of Canada, "Public Accounts of Canada: Annual Report of Parliament on Crown Corporations and Other Corporate Interests of Canada", Ottawa, various dates.

TREBILCOCK, M.J., *et. al.,* "The Choice of Governing Instrument", Ottawa, ECC, 1982.

VERNON, Raymond and Yair AHARONI, eds,. "State-Owned Enterprise in the Western Economies", London, 1981.

World Bank, "Bureaucrats in Business: The Economics and Politics of Government Ownership", Oxford, 1995.

HOW DO EMPLOYEES OWN THEIR WORKPLACE?

by
Brendan Martin[*]
Public World, London

1.   Introductory summary

This paper explores the relationship between employee ownership and corporate governance and concludes that 'ownership' in a metaphorical sense -- associated with claims to influence over corporate decisions deriving from employment rights rather than property rights -- has more significant impact than ownership in the literal sense. By reference to examples drawn from a mixture of primary research, the literature and previous OECD conferences, the paper suggests that there is wide variety in the circumstances and effects of employee ownership in the literal sense and that the interests of employees involved in buy-outs can be heterogeneous. It concludes that arrangements for employees' 'ownership' of corporate decisions in the metaphorical sense has more bearing on their influence in corporate governance than their ownership of shares, and suggests that industrial democracy of that kind can also contribute positively to successful restructuring and gains in efficiency and quality.

2.   What do workers want to own?

A small Swedish municipality contracted out several technical services, including roads maintenance, water supply and property caretaking. The company which won the contract took on about 120 of the staff previously employed by the local authority. After three years:

  - The tasks previously carried out by the technical management division are now being carried out equally well by the contractors

---

*   Brendan Martin is a consultant to Public Services International and the Trade Union Advisory Committee to the OECD.

at lower cost and on the basis of a more efficient decision-making process.

–   The staff say that their duties are now more interesting, that they have greater decision-making responsibilities, that they enjoy their work more, that they are better paid and that channels for transmission of decisions are shorter.

–   A number of employees felt that they had been short-changed by their union. They have now been working for the contractor for three years and take a completely different view of their employer than does the union. Here is one of their comments: "The biggest threat hanging over us today is that of having to go back to working for the local authority. We feel we have more freedom at work now."[1]

The words of a politician or private business leader, promoting municipal privatisation against labour union opposition? No. That was, in fact, the candid account of a leader of the Swedish municipal employees' union SKTF. This paper reproduces those words not because they describe the aftermath of management or employee buy-out -- they do not -- nor because they typify the results of contracting-out -- they do not -- but because of the insight they offer into some of the key issues for many employees in the context of post-privatisation corporate governance, but which can be concealed from both their employers and their unions by stereotyped views of what matters to workers.

Better pay has, of course, always been a staple of organised labour, but consider those other matters in the second paragraph of that quotation: more interesting duties, more say in decision making, more enjoyment of their jobs, both through what they do and through the satisfaction of working for a more efficient organisation. Those and related issues are less traditional but increasingly common components of what employees in OECD countries want at work and of what their labour unions are trying to achieve on their members' behalf.

That is not to say that employees are disinterested in opportunities to share in the ownership of the enterprises by which they are employed, or that ownership in that conventional sense cannot serve 'ownership' in the metaphorical sense. But it is to distinguish between them and to consider which sense of 'ownership' really affords more involvement in corporate governance.

There are those who will protest that ownership without property rights is meaningless, or even downright dangerous, and proof of the necessity for as much privatisation as possible in order to install a real owner and stop public employees behaving as if they own the place. There is no denying that some public employees in many countries, and many in some, have exercised illegitimate authority against the public interest. However, this should not blind us to the existence of a sphere of legitimate authority for employees at all levels in their workplace -- whether public or private -- or to the fact that this sphere clearly does imply limits to and compromise with authority deriving from property rights. Moreover, many owners and managers, in both public and private sectors, believe strongly that in order to achieve effective restructuring and reorganisation to improve efficiency and quality, their employees must believe in those changes and feel they have an investment in them. Such a commitment on the part of employees is sometimes referred to -- significantly, perhaps -- as 'ownership' of the changes that need to be made, regardless of whether or not those employees have property rights in the enterprise.

These points are linguistically demanding in English but much more so in translation to other languages. The difficulty in German of distinguishing between 'shareholder' and 'stakeholder' demonstrates the problem (and is curious given that Germany more than many countries seems to make that distinction itself in the way it organises its economy and social affairs). In the UK and perhaps some other countries, the term stakeholder as opposed to shareholder is recognised as differentiating between those with property rights and those with stakes of other kinds arising from their economic relationship with the company -- customers and suppliers, as well as employees. In the context of this presentation, the key distinctions are summarised in the following representation.

Employee ownership	Employee 'ownership'
shares	stakes
property rights	employment rights
share value	basic pay and conditions
dividend	performance rewards
board representation,	collective bargaining,
AGM,	consultation,
sale of shares	board representation

The point of the above is to demonstrate that acquisition of ownership share in the property sense is not the employee's only source of rights in corporate governance, because employment rights imply some minimum level of say in corporate affairs and can extend even as far as board representation. In terms of rewards, likewise, there can be incentives linked to the overall success of the company or to individual performance which do not rely on share ownership.

3.   Employee share ownership and pay

If we look at some examples of employee share ownership and its relationship with corporate governance in the context of privatisation we shall see that it is quite possible that 'ownership' deriving from employment rights affords employees more say in the direction of their employing organisation than ownership rights deriving from property rights. (Indeed, you could even say that ownership rights deriving from employment are more important than property rights derived from shareholding. In fact, there is evidence to suggest that employee share ownership undermines the collective exercise of employment rights through unions. For example, the record of union organisation in US companies with Employee Share Ownership Plans (ESOPs) is very low.)

Martin Mayer combines roles as a manual worker, a trade union representative, a shareholder *and* a director of Mainline Buses in the English city of Sheffield. Mainline was privatised through a 100% employee buy-out of a particularly equitable kind. However, describing his experience of his colleagues' attitudes to pay and conditions, Mayer says:

> 'Ownership doesn't give you control of the company ... at the end of the day, whether you have a share stake in the company or not, what really matters is not that, it's your wages and conditions.'[2]

And, indeed, industrial action by Mayer's members against the company they overwhelmingly own is currently threatened. That does not appear to be typical, but might not be unusual either. One study of privatisations in Poland found workers determined to take early advantage of abolition of wage controls. 'Apparently, the small shareholdings held by workers are not felt to be significant enough to overshadow their interests as wage-earners.'[3] However, other commentators from that country have suggested that employee share ownership has served to encourage pay restraint.[4] From Hungary, one important study of post-privatisation performance of enterprises privatised through management and/or employee buy-outs has found:

'As the share of employees' incomes made up by dividends and any capital gains was insignificant, the focus of employees' attention was on receiving higher wages and keeping their jobs. However, as the firms generally had substantial debts and little funding available for investment, employees generally accepted relatively low wage increases.'[5]

Workers at Kardemir steel works in Turkey settled for no pay increase in the first year after becoming 35% owners by investing the redundancy money they received when the state washed its hands of their failing and overstaffed enterprise. Their plant was in such dire need of investment, restructuring and rationalisation that it had been written off not only by the government but also by international institutions such as the World Bank. The pay freeze in the year after the buy-out meant that the employees' real income that year effectively fell by about 40%. The workers knew, however, that the alternative was closure and the loss of all their jobs in a region which offered few alternative prospects for employment.

Similarly in the United Kingdom, according to Willie Coupar, who became managing director of the Chesterfield Transport bus company having been a labour union representative of the employees there before privatisation:

'Substantial improvements in profitability have been achieved over the last three years. Staff have contributed enormously to this through major changes in working practices. At the time of the buy-out we were quite unequivocal about profits being the main priority. Everything else had to be secondary because without an adequate return, the company's short and long term prosperity would clearly be jeopardised. Many of the toughest decisions we have taken could be termed "people versus profit" decisions.'[6]

At Mainline Buses, the experience has been rather different, although, according to union convenor Peter Briggs, the information rights conveyed by the employee shares trust has produced a more open disclosure regime. He still does not entirely trust the accuracy of numbers provided by management, but does concede:

'It's given us something we haven't had before and that's dialogue with the directors over the nuts and bolts of running the business and the strategy and budget. We never had that before. Before, our only representation was on the trade union and when we came to talk to management about wages they might tell us what's going on with the company and why they can't afford to pay us, but we've never really been involved in how they got to that decision, so we felt remote from that.[7]

However, another senior union representative at Mainline says this has not stopped them pushing hard to improve terms and conditions, although, he says, union strategy on pay has changed, with negotiators now taking a more positive view of performance-related pay and pressing for non-financial benefits such as free bus passes for employees' spouses.

4.   Employee share ownership and jobs

The evidence as to the impact of employee ownership on employee pay demands and bargaining is, therefore inconclusive and suggests that employee ownership may not be as significant an influence on wage levels as prevailing market conditions, union strength and other variables. Similarly, it is not possible to infer from the fact that employment protection is a motivating factor in employees taking ownership stakes through privatisation that they will use their ownership rights to prevent restructuring which threatens jobs. Indeed, there is some evidence and strong argument to the contrary. To quote a paper by Professor Leroy Jones of Boston University given at a meeting of the OECD advisory group on privatisation:

> 'Typically workers are guaranteed some combination of freedom from layoffs for a specified period, concessional share ownership, and/or guaranteed maintenance of relative wages. In return, unions relax the onerous work rules which preclude efficiency gains. The result, with better management and incentives, can be rapid reduction in unit costs and expansion of output. Even if enterprises are overstaffed by, say, 30%, natural attrition and rising output can eliminate the excess employment in a few years.'[8]

That view was supported by another paper at the same meeting by Iosef Bakaleynik, general director and chairman of the Vladimir Tractor Works, who said the employees group -- owners of 40% of the shares -- were 'actively involved in management' and commented:

> 'I believe that the participation of employees is to the benefit of the enterprise -- it is not a bad thing. They should participate in decisions in their division, where they know the situation best of all. They must feel their voice is heard.'

Significantly, however, Bakaleynik commented that the employees allowed their managers to exercise their authority by proxy, presumably in the tacit belief that their managers knew better than they how to secure the enterprise's future and with it their employment security.

Similarly, at Chesterfield Transport, says Willie Coupar:

'There can be no doubt that in Chesterfield Transport most employees subscribed for shares in the company to safeguard their jobs and conditions. At the same time, it would be wrong to imply that employees felt that their shareholding was in some sense a guarantee of employment. Rather, employee share ownership was seen as a safeguard for their company and their personal security against outside predators.'

5.   Employee ownership and restructuring

In other cases, however, employee ownership has not produced such a corporatist mentality. Again, the experience of Mainline Buses in Sheffield is instructive. Despite the majority shareholding of the employees there, worker-director Martin Mayer says:

'There is still a them and us, but it's been exacerbated for other reasons outside the ESOP. The them and us comes from the fact the company is now private, the management are very much in the driving seat and they have got a huge responsibility in trying to make the company work under very, very difficult conditions. I respect that, that is true. I don't necessarily think they are terribly good managers and what is the easiest thing in the world when you're not really making much money but to come and try to cut costs and if you're going to do that how do you do that nicely and take everyone on board? Well, it's very difficult, isn't it?'

The division thus expressed is in sharp contrast to developments at Welsh Water, another privatised company in the UK, where managers and employees (with the help of unions) have developed an agreement called Partnership for Progress which has evolved over the last six years and now involves a set of mutual commitments. The company has committed itself to:

- employment security through a no compulsory redundancy guarantee

- maintenance of pay levels through a 'fair pay formula'

- profit-related pay

- single status employment conditions

- skills development and training programmes

- increasing involvement of employees in management and greater authority for self-management

- welfare initiatives

- equal opportunities

In return, the employees have collectively committed themselves to:

- strive for consistently high levels of personal performance

- enjoy and feel positive about their work

- co-operate with changes to improve efficiency

- flexibility

- learn new skills

- take on new responsibilities

After a visit to Welsh Water, Bill Jordan, then president of the engineering workers union in Britain, commented:

> Management is talking with the workforce and the unions about the problems they face [...] I'm going to market what I've seen and take it around the country as an example and try to get others to follow.[9]

That testimony, given in 1993, might have some international significance now, because Jordan has since become general secretary of the International Confederation of Free Trade Unions.

Welsh Water is the only privatised UK water company taking such an approach to management - at least one other has taken a much more aggressive approach by derecognising unions. There was no element of management or employee buy-out in the way in which Welsh Water was privatised, although throughout the sector, in common with other UK privatisations, preferential shares were made available to employees. So its partnership approach would appear to have nothing to do with either employee ownership or privatisation in themselves, but with a propensity to a participative rather than adversarial approach to management and industrial relations on the part of executives and labour representatives there. Again, these examples suggest that factors other than the existence or extent of employee ownership have more influence over worker attitudes to corporate governance.

In the case of Chesterfield Transport, Willie Coupar himself stresses that, while employee ownership might have been a necessary condition for securing the workforce's support for restructuring, it certainly was not a sufficient condition. In any event, the paradox is that buy-outs in the context of bus privatisation in United Kingdom have in fact failed to provide the 'security against outside predators' which Coupar says was the Chesterfield employees' goal. Rather, the majority of buy-outs have proved to be a transitory form of post-privatisation ownership, with equity and debt holders eventually exiting through trade sales or often highly lucrative flotations. This has led to rapid consolidation of the UK bus industry, which is now more than 50% controlled by four companies.

That experience parallels that of employee ownership in the context of privatisation in Russia and, to a lesser extent, other transition countries, where sales to employees have been a device to overcome immediate political or ideological resistance to privatisation, or to undermine labour opposition, but has been followed by concentration of ownership, either with insiders or through take-overs or institutional accumulation. According to Leroy Jones, commenting on a World Bank study of 12 privatisation cases in which he was a research leader:

> 'The case studies suggested that it is not a myth that the public enterprise wage bill is bloated, but that some of the gains from privatisation can be used to buy workers' support. In fact, at least in mixed economies which are not extremely hard authoritarian states, such an arrangement is a pre-condition to level one success: without it, the enterprise will not be sold.' [10]

So what determines whether companies privatised by sales to management and employees are the predator or the victim three or four years down the line, or whether, indeed, they survive in any form? This may well have less to do with their post-privatisation governance than with their condition at the time of privatisation. While many a company in good financial condition has been privatised with major or minor employee ownership for the political or labour relations reasons mentioned above, in some cases -- including the Turkish case of Kardemir -- it has been a last resort before closure. Therefore, enterprise failure would not necessarily be a failure primarily of corporate governance -- surviving for as long as three years could be a triumph against the odds.

6.   The heterogeneous nature of employee ownership

A further reason to avoid over-generalising about the impact of employee ownership on corporate governance is simply that 'employee ownership' can mean many things, and does not necessarily imply a unity of interests among employees but can even imply the reverse. It can mean everything from 100% employee ownership and equal but small stakes for each employee, as at Mainline, to a takeover by a handful of senior managers, with or without a smaller stake for other employees. Therefore, incentives also vary greatly. Senior managers and other employees at a train leasing company in Britain last month realised fabulous gains when the company was sold just over a year after it was privatised. For the chairman, that brought a return worth more than $4m for an equity investment of the equivalent of $40 000 at the time of privatisation 13 months earlier. His governance of the firm must indeed have been wondrous to bring about so rapid an improvement in its financial fortunes. His employees are not complaining about the same rapid increase in the value of their shares -- employee members of the share trust which invested about $150 000 on behalf of 66 workers will now receive about that much each -- but whether or not their interests will be as well served as their chairman's have been by the firm's take-over may depend on whether they keep their jobs as well as their windfall.

Nor do even front-line employees necessarily have common interests. Three years ago, Malcolm Morgan, a bus driver in the south of England earning the equivalent of about $15 000 a year received a windfall of about $300 000 when his acquisitive company, which had taken over many rivals and greatly expanded its territory, went public. Before privatisation, he worked an eight-hour day with a co-driver. Since privatisation he works a 12-hour day on his own. The fate of the other drivers whose jobs disappeared tends to be less well-publicised than the good fortune of the Malcolm Morgans and the much better fortunes of their senior managers.

A further example comes from Mexico, where, according to a study by the International Labour Organisation, while a small percentage of the shares of the privatised telecommunications company Telmex was distributed equally between the employees, the burden of restructuring fell on them far from equally, with some departments having to deal with very rapid change, job cuts and flexibility, while others were hardly affected. It seems from the ILO account that, even if they did own a few shares, the Telmex employees certainly didn't feel that they "owned" the changes sweeping around them, and that they felt alienated from their unions as well as from their management as a result. This might not be healthy for the company's industrial relations and performance in the future.

7.   Employee 'ownership' of workplace change

This theme brings us back to the Swedish public service example quoted earlier. The public service unions in that country have learned from experience that a more effective response to the restructuring of the organisations employing their members than opposition is to themselves advocate and design changes in the workplace. These changes are designed to achieve simultaneously four objectives which some regard as mutually incompatible -- lower costs, higher quality, employment security and increased job satisfaction. One union, SKAF, has gone so far as to set up a special consultancy division, called Komanco. The official in charge of the programme has explained:

> 'In order to confront requests for cuts in public services or privatisation, SKAF has realised that just trying to refuse changes is not very constructive, especially as some of the accusations of inefficiency in the public services have definitely been true. SKAF has for many years stressed that the traditional hierarchical organisation of work in local government administration must by necessity be inefficient if it does not involve the knowledge and experience of the employees.'

> 'We started to develop a model to build more efficient, non-hierarchical organisations by involving the employees, with the aim of saving money without making people redundant. Our ideas were tested in 1991 in one municipality -- Malung. The goal was to decrease costs by at least 10% within three years. Already in 1992, Malung had saved 10.5 per cent.'[11]

Since then Komanco has sold its approach to 60 other Swedish municipalities. The model consists basically of decentralised team building and collective employee self-regulation to achieve negotiated results in terms of quality and efficiency. It is not a standard package but depends on working with each particular group of employees to draw solutions out of them and leave them feeling that they 'own' those plans.

While formal ownership stakes or other forms of financial reward are not necessarily prior conditions for effectively involving employees in improving corporate governance, they may well be the conditions to sustain that involvement in the long term as the workers begin to expect their success to be more tangibly rewarded than by increased job satisfaction alone. Recognition and reward for past achievement can become critical to sustaining and building upon that achievement, although the role of financial incentives as a precondition for co-operation has been exaggerated. There is evidence, indeed, that financial incentives can be counter-productive.[12]

8.   The developing bargaining agenda

The way in which union bargaining agendas are developing internationally reinforces the impression that 'ownership' - in the metaphorical sense of having greater say in the immediate and long-term development of their working environment - is of more importance to employees than ownership in the literal, property sense. The ideal would no doubt be a combination of ownership in both senses, but the evidence does not suggest there is a causal connection between the two.

The trends can be seen as follows:

The developing bargaining agenda

Not only	**Employment**	*But also*	**Job satisfaction**
	Security		**Responsibility**
	Bargaining rights		**Employee empowerment**
	Fair pay and terms		**Share of rewards**
Reconciling:	**Lower costs, higher quality, security, better jobs**		

The two columns should not be seen as alternatives. The increasing willingness of labour unions to negotiate and even initiate changes in work organisation which increase job flexibility is typically premised on agreed employment security. Conversely, lack of employment security tends to

144

reinforce rigidity in the deployment of employees, since it builds in restrictive practices incentives. While labour is increasingly committed to working with employers to increase competitiveness -- and many employers are seeing the advantages of such a partnership approach -- the bottom line in such co-operation is fair pay and conditions. In the same way, moves towards greater consultation, involvement and representation of employees in corporate governance decisions, not only at plant level but at national and international company levels, is seen as a complement rather than an alternative to union recognition.

The development of the latter concept is being expressed on an international level in the growing use of works councils as forums for enterprise-level 'social partnership'. This development is clearly driven in part in the European Union by legal requirements arising form the Maastricht Treaty, but some companies -- such as transnational cleaning contractor ISS -- have exceeded legal obligations and recognised unions as a matter of what the company views as sound industrial relations practice.

9.   New forms of employee ownership and corporate governance

Other developments of union activity might point to a much more important future relationship between employee ownership (in the property sense) and corporate governance than can be seen so far in relation to buy-outs or ESOPs. First, unions, like other civil society organisations, are becoming increasingly adept at public relations and, in particular, at using access to company AGMs for campaigning purposes. For example, unions representing British gas workers paraded a live pig outside the annual general meeting of British Gas as a headline-grabbing protest about executive pay and share options in the UK's privatised utilities. The stunt found resonance not only with public opinion but perhaps more importantly with institutional investors who were also becoming fed up with executive sui-generosity, and it was not long afterwards that the company's chief executive stepped down. Second, unions in some countries -- notably South Africa -- are setting up their own investment funds, and in the case of South Africa the fund owned by an airline workers' union has been collaborating with Virgin Airlines in the development of a plan to buy a domestic airline, Sun Air, which is to be privatised. Thirdly, some unions are taking an increasing interest in the way in which their members' pension funds are deployed, not only to protect the value of those funds and prevent their abuse but also to serve other union objectives and employee interests through investment decisions.

Interesting though such developments are, and significant though they might become, they should not be overstated. Employee share ownership has certainly played an important part in privatisation but, in the transition countries, for example, there is already widespread disappointment about its capacity to really protect and promote workers' interests. We are likely to see instead the assertion or reassertion of the more conventional means of employee organisation and influence on corporate governance -- that is, employees exercising the pursuit of their collective interest through labour unions or other means. In transition countries, at this stage that means mainly the development of the basic institutions of industrial relations and basic bargaining issues -- wages and conditions, previously determined by state -- as both private employers and employees develop their capacity and know-how in an evolving legal and regulatory framework.

The way in which those institutions work, and the environment in which they work, is likely to have more influence on corporate governance in most cases for the foreseeable future than are institutions of employee share ownership. However, as they are increasingly complemented by the emergence of new managerial approaches to employee involvement, both industrial relations and the role of employees in corporate governance seem likely to show gradual change.

NOTES

1.   Quoted in In the Public Interest? Privatisation and Public Sector Reform, Brendan Martin, Zed Books, London, 1993.

2.   Personal interview, February 1997.

3.   'The Managerial Revolution Revisited: The Case of Privatisation in Poland', Jacek Tittenbrun, in Capital & Class, No. 55, p.24.

4.   This point was made by Minister Freyberg during the conference.

5.   Buy-outs in Hungary, Poland and Russia: governance and finance issues', Igor Filatotchev, Irena Grosfeld, Judit Karsai, Mike Wright, Trevor Buck, in Economics of Transition, Vol.4 (1), 1996, p.71.

6.   'Employee buy-out brings changes on the buses', William Coupar, in Involvement & Partnership, No. 617, 1993.

7.   Personal interview, February 1997.

8.   Leroy Jones, *op cit*.

9.   Quoted in Putting it into Practice, Number 3, Involvement and Participation Association, London, 1996.

10.   Paper by Leroy Jones to OECD Advisory Group On Privatisation, Moscow, March 1995.

11.   Quoted in European Integration And Modernisation of Local Public Services: Trade Union Responses And Initiatives, Brendan Martin, EPSU, Brussels, 1996.

12.   See the present author's report on performance-related pay in UK public services for the DGB EGöD 2000 project, DGB, Düsseldorf, October 1996.

OECD PUBLICATIONS, 2, rue André-Pascal, 75775 PARIS CEDEX 16
PRINTED IN FRANCE
(21 98 03 1 P) ISBN 92-64-16075-2 – No. 50091 1998